The Fragments of Heraclitus:

Greek Text with Vocabulary, Grammar, and Commentary

by Matthew R. Blain

TABLE OF CONTENTS

First Edition

ISBN: 979-8-218-22281-9

PREFACE

In every translation, some aspect or nuance of a writing is unfortunately lost. In the worst of them, everything is lost. Friedrich Schlegel, the Romantic-era German philosopher and poet, once wrote in his notebooks:

> "What is lost in average, good, or even first-rate translations is
> precisely the best part."[i]

The only way to avoid loss in translation is to read an author in their original voice, with a patience to appreciate the nuance of their word-choice, style, and context. Languages do not have a 1-to-1 correspondence between them. That kind of presumption inhibits an ability to appreciate the subtlety and nuance of a text. Much like puns, witticisms, or tongue-in-cheek remarks in English, specific ancient Greek words maintain a subtlety and depth that can be easily lost in translation. On the lighter side, Heraclitus makes a pun between βίος (life) and βιός (bow), highlighting how one's duty is death and the other's is life, though both use the same word. This pun is not only word play, but also indicative of one of Heraclitus' central themes, referred to by scholars as the unity of opposites. However, this is but one of the many profound themes in Heraclitus' *oeuvre*, including those of flux and the all-pervading λόγος.

This commentary aims to provide the keys to one of the most profound, albeit cryptic, Pre-Socratic thinkers in his own words. These keys to Heraclitus are twofold: the first of which is to provide ease of access to beginning and intermediate Greek students in translating Heraclitus and the second being to facilitate individual study or group discussion on Heraclitus' enigmatic fragments. By already doing the preliminary dictionary and grammatical research, this work removes this burden from potential readers of Heraclitus.[1] By doing so, this commentary

---

[1] I would be remiss if I claimed to have provided an exhaustive definition for each Greek word. In interpreting more obscure fragments, I highly recommend consulting a more in-depth dictionary such as the Liddell-Scott-Jones

will allow for more extended discussions of the philosophical insights and Greek with which he writes instead of wasting more time turning through dictionaries, scouring internet databases, or debating grammatical devices. However, this text will not merely spoon-feed insights into the philosophy and understanding of Heraclitus, but, instead, shall pave the way for students to contemplate the complexity of Heraclitean aphorisms more easily, bolstering both their knowledge of Ancient Greek, and appreciation of the rich Pre-Socratic wisdom.

Heraclitus is notoriously esoteric and difficult; however, Diogenes Laertius tells us that Heraclitus intentionally crafted his fragments to be obscure and difficult, claiming that only those who would be worthy or strong enough (δυνάμενοι) should approach his work.[ii]

Lexicon for the most nuanced and thorough definitions, references, and citations of specific words in other historical contexts.

Note on the Text Itself

Heraclitus' Περὶ Φύσεως is yet another unfortunate loss in the history of Western thinking. However, the following 126 fragments of Heraclitus in this volume are those that have been rediscovered across dozens of works as doxa or direct citation and then arranged in the order corresponding to the Dielz-Kranz numbering system from the 1903 edition of *Die Fragmente Der Vorsokratiker*. To this same end, there is a letter "B" before the number of each fragment since the DK listing's "A" fragments only pertain to quotes biographically about a certain Pre-Socratic's life while the "B" fragments are those attributed to the thinker in question. I have included the "B" before each number in my listing in order to make this distinction as clear and specific as possible. For additional information regarding the individual sources of each of the following fragments and additional elaborations by the respective source, I highly recommend browsing the latest edition of *Die Fragmente Der Vorsokratiker*, the proper citation of which can be found in the bibliography.

With the exception of fragments 4, 37, and 106 which are preserved in Latin, the remaining fragments are preserved in the Greek found in *Die Fragmente Der Vorsokratiker* with additional consulting and cross-referencing of John Burnet's *Early Greek Philosophy*, T.M. Robinson's, and Henry Johnstone' versions of the text, among others. Cross-referencing and editing down the unabridged fragments from *Die Fragmente Der Vorsokratiker* allow for the most accurate presentation of Heraclitus' extant thought. However, I have left some fragments with their dicta (in grey) that can provide some additional context as to what the writer who cited Heraclitus was thinking or mentioning at the time of citing him.

Note on the Vocabulary and Grammar Notes

For any and all of the vocabulary provided in the notes for all the text provided below, I have made great use of the seventh edition of Liddell and Scott's authoritative *An Intermediate Greek-English Lexicon*. Utilizing the 1940 edition, it has provided the near entirety of the definitions below due to its thorough index of Epic, Doric, Attic, and Ionic Greek dialects and their related forms, the latter two of which were most necessary to distinguish for this edition.

In the notes provided for each fragment, I have included, when proper, an endnote with a citation to a specific section in Smythe's *Greek Grammar* as an additional reference to the point in question. For example, such notes are present in more nuanced Greek points such as adverbial accusatives (5), epexegetical use of ἤ in an indirect question (30), or datives of reference (107), among others. In addition to grammar and syntax, other endnotes cite either to other authors/commentators or additional contextual/historical information for the fragment in question.

Differences Between Ancient Ionic and Attic Greek

Being from Ephesus and having flourished around 500 B.C., Heraclitus wrote, with the exception of the fragments recovered only in Latin, in the Ionic dialect.[iii] Thankfully, the differences in morphology and form are not so different or daunting that they should discourage any beginner or intermediate Greek student, regardless of whether one has grown accustomed to Attic, Koine, or Homeric.

The following chart provides some of the discrepancies of Ionic compared to Attic:

Change		Attic	Ionic
Consonant Change: π to κ		ὅπως	ὅκως
		ὁπόσα	ὁκόσα
		ὁπόταν	ὁκόταν
		ὅπη	ὅκη
Resolution of Diphthongs and Contractions	α = ηι	ἡμέρᾳ	ἡμέρηι
	αῖς = ῆισι(ν)	ψυχαῖς	ψυχῇσιν
	ια = ιη	πολυμαθία	πολυμαθίη
		ἁρμονία	ἁρμονίη
		σκολιά	σκολιή
		ὑγίεια	ὑγιείη
		σοφία	σοφίη
		πυρκαιάν	πυρκαϊήν
	α = η	λύρα	λύρη
	εια = ηιη	βασιλεία	βασιληίη
Switching of the Aspirate Consonant		αὖθις	αὖτις
Ionic Greek Sometimes Retains Uncontracted rather than Contracted Forms (Hadley 157D)	Verbs	διαχεῖται	διαχέεται
		μετρεῖται	μετρέεται
		δοκοῦντα	δοκέοντα
	Nouns	νοῦς	νόος

This chart is by no means exhaustive of every difference found between the two dialects but merely demonstrative of the most prominent discrepancies found in Heraclitus' extant fragments. For more on Ionic Greek grammar, the bibliography contains some excellent sources, some of which are easily accessible in the public domain for additional reference.

If the reader notices any discrepancies, mistakes, or other errors in this text and commentary, please reach out to me at MatthewRBlain@Gmail.com so that I can quickly edit the manuscript and update it online. It is greatly appreciated.

Matthew R. Blain

List of Abbreviations Used Within this Commentary

Absolute	Abs.	Indirect Question	IQ
Accusative	Acc.	Indirect Statement	IS
Active	Act.	Infinitive	Inf.
Adjective	Adj.	Liddell-Scott Jones Dictionary	LSJ
Adverb	Adv.	Masculine	M.
Antecedent	Ante.	Middle	Midd.
Aorist	Aor.	Neuter	N.
Article	Art.	Nominative	Nom.
Articular Inf.	AI	Object	Obj.
Circumstantial	Circum.	Optative	Opt.
Comparative	Comp.	Participle	Part.
Conjunction	Conj.	Passive	Pass.
Contract	Contr.	Perfect	Perf.
Contrary-to-Fact	CTF	Pluperfect	Plup.
Correlatives	Correl.	Plural	Pl.
Dative	Dat.	Predicate	Pred.
Demonstrative	Demon.	Preposition	Prep.
Feminine	F.	Present	Pres.
Future	Fut.	Present General Condition	PGC
Future Less Vivid	FLV	Pronoun	Pro.
Future More Vivid	FMV	Relative	Rel.
Genitive	Gen.	Singular	Sg.
Hortatory	Hort.	Subject	Sub.
Imperative	Imp.	Subjunctive	Subj.
Imperfect	Impf.	Superlative	Superl.
Indicative	Ind.	Verb Person	1st, 2nd, 3rd

Bibliography

~ Asterisk (*) indicates that the work is in the Public Domain ~

Translations and Texts of Heraclitus

*Burnet, John. *Early Greek Philosophy*, 2nd Edition. London: Adam and Charles Black, 1908.

Davenport, Guy. *Herakleitos and Diogenes*. San Francisco, CA: Grey Fox Press, 1979.

*Diels, Hermann. *Die fragmente der Vorsokratiker Griechisch und Deutsch*. Berlin:
Weidmann, 1903

Diels, Hermann, and Walther Kranz. *Die Fragmente der Vorsokratiker* (*The Fragments of
the Pre-Socratics*), 6th Edition. Weidmann: Zürich, 1951.

Haxton, Brooks. *Fragments: The Collected Wisdom of Heraclitus*. Penguin Group USA, 2001.

Kirk, G. S.; Raven, J. & Schofield, Malcolm. *The Presocratic Philosophers: A Critical History
with a Selection of Texts*. Cambridge University Press, 1983.

Graham, Daniel W. *The Texts of Early Greek Philosophy: The Complete Fragments and Selected
Testimonies of the Major Presocratics*. New York, NY: Cambridge University Press,
2010.

Lebedev, A.V. *The Logos of Heraclitus. A Reconstruction of his Word and Thought. (With a New
Critical Edition of the Fragments)*. Saint Petersburg, Nauka, 2014.

*Patrick, G.T.W. *The Fragments of Heraclitus*. Baltimore, MD: N. Murray, 1889.

Robinson, T.M. 1991. *Heraclitus: Fragments : A Text and Translation with a Commentary*.
Toronto: University of Toronto Press, 1987.

Sweet, Dennis. *Heraclitus: Translation and Analysis*. University Press of America, 2007.

Wheelwright, Philip Ellis. *Heraclitus*. Princeton, New Jersey: Princeton University Press, 1959.

Philological Aids and Reference Works

*Fisk, Benjamin-Franklin. *A Grammar of the Greek Language*. Boston, MA: Hilliard, Grey, and

Company, 1836. https://shorturl.at/oAOU4

*Lewis, Charlton T. and Charles Short. *A New Latin Dictionary*. Oxford: Clarendon Press, 1891.

Liddell, Henry George, Robert Scott, Henry Stuart Jones, and Roderick McKenzie. *A Greek-

English Lexicon New ed*. Oxford: Clarendon Press, 1940.

*Smyth, Herbert Weir. *A Greek Grammar for Colleges*. New York, NY: American Book

Company, 1920.

https://archive.org/details/agreekgrammarfo02smytgoog/page/n19/mode/1up

*Smyth, Herbert Weir. *The Sounds and Inflections of the Greek Dialects: Ionic*. Oxford:

Clarendon Press, 1894.

https://archive.org/details/soundsinflection00smytrich/page/n7/mode/2up

Philosophical Interpretations of Heraclitus

Brann, Eva. *The Logos of Heraclitus*. Philadelphia, PA: Paul Dry Books, 2011.

Graham, Daniel W., "Heraclitus", The Stanford Encyclopedia of Philosophy (Summer 2021 Edition), Edward N. Zalta (ed.).

Heidegger, Martin. *Heraclitus Seminar*. Translated by Frank Eugen. United States: Northwestern University Press, 1993.

Heidegger, Martin. *Heraclitus: The Inception of Occidental Thinking and Logic: Heraclitus's Doctrine of the Logos*. Translated by Julia Goesser Assiante and S. Montgomery Ewegen New York, NY: Bloomsbury Academic, 2018.

Kahn, Charles H. *The Art and Thought of Heraclitus: A New Arrangement and Translation of the Fragments with Literary and Philosophical Commentary*. Cambridge: Cambridge University Press, 1979. doi:10.1017/CBO9780511627392.

Kirk, G.S.. *Heraclitus: The Cosmic Fragments*. Cambridge: Cambridge University Press, 1954.

Jaspers, Karl. *Anaximander, Heraclitus, Parmenides, Plotinus, Lao-Tzu, Nagarjuna*. Edited by Hanna Arendt and Translated by Ralph Manheim. New York, NY: A Helen and Kurt Wolff Book, 1966

Nietzsche, Friedrich. *Philosophy in the Tragic Age of the Greeks*. Translated by Marianne Cowan. Washington, D.C.: Regnery Publishing, Inc., 1962.

"His [Heraclitus] has, on the whole, a bent towards a philosophy of nature, for the principle, although logical, is apprehended as the universal nature-process."

- G.W.F. Hegel[iv]

"In Heraclitus we see the perfection of knowledge so far as it has gone, a perfecting of the Idea into a totality, which is the beginning of Philosophy, since it expresses the essence of the Idea, the Notion of the infinite, the potentially and actively existent, as that which it is, i.e. as the unity of opposites. From Heraclitus dates the ever-remaining Idea which is the same in all philosophers to the present day, as it was the Idea of Plato and of Aristotle."

- G.W.F. Hegel[v]

"He does not grow: I mean, philosophy does not follow the course of the other sciences, even if certain of the philosopher's territories gradually fall into the hands of science. Heraclitus can never be obsolete. Philosophy is invention beyond the limits of experience; it is the continuation of the mythical drive."

- Friedrich Nietzsche[vi vii]

"Among the most ancient Greek thinkers, it is Heraclitus who was subjected to the most fundamentally un-Greek misinterpretation in the course of Western history, and who nevertheless in more recent times has provided the strongest impulses toward redisclosing what is authentically Greek."
- Martin Heidegger[viii]

13

ΗΡΑΚΛΕΙΤΟΥ ΠΕΡΙ ΦΥΣΕΩΣ

B 1

1.1 δὲ λόγου τοῦδ' ἐόντος ἀεὶ ἀξύνετοι γίνονται ἄνθρωποι καὶ πρόσθεν ἢ ἀκοῦσαι καὶ
1.2 ἀκούσαντες τὸ πρῶτον· γινομένων γὰρ πάντων κατὰ τὸν λόγον τόνδε ἀπείροισιν
1.3 ἐοίκασι, πειρώμενοι καὶ ἐπέων καὶ ἔργων τοιούτων, ὁκοίων ἐγὼ διηγεῦμαι κατὰ
1.4 φύσιν διαιρέων ἕκαστον καὶ φράζων ὅκως ἔχει. τοὺς δὲ ἄλλους ἀνθρώπους λανθάνει
1.5 ὁκόσα ἐγερθέντες ποιοῦσιν, ὅκωσπερ ὁκόσα εὕδοντες ἐπιλανθάνονται.

ἀεὶ: (Adv.) always, ever

ἀκούω: to hear something (+Acc.); to hear from/of someone (+Gen.)

ἄλλος, -η, -ον: another, one besides; (w/Article) the rest, the others

ἄνθρωπος,-ου, ὁ: man, human, person

ἀξύνετος, -ον: witless, devoid of understanding, not able to understand

ἄπειρος, -ον: without trial, unused to, unacquainted to

γὰρ: (Conj.) for, since

γίγνομαι: become, come into being, be born, be produced

δὲ: (Particle) but, and

διαιρέω: to take apart, divide into parts; determine, divide among themselves

διηγέομαι: to set out in detail, describe

ἐγείρω: to awaken, rouse, stir up

ἐγώ: I

ἕκαστος, -η, -ον: each, every

ἔοικα: Perf. Act. form translated in a Pres. Aspect; to seem, be like (+ Dat.)

εἰμί: to be

ἔπος, ἔπους, τὸ: word, (as opposed to deed), speech, poetry, story,

ἐπιλανθάνομαι: to forget

ἔργον, -ου, τό: deed, action, labor, work

εὕδω: to sleep

ἔχω: to have, hold

ἤ: (Conj.) or

καί: (Conj.) and, even, also

κατά: (+Acc.) according to, corresponding with

λανθάνω: to escape notice, escape

λόγος, -ου, ὁ: best to leave it as λόγος (or) as word, account, reason, understanding

ὁκοῖος, -α, -ον: of what sort

ὁπόσος, -η, -ον: as many/much as; (In Indirect Questions) however much, however many

ὅπως: (Adv.) as, in such manner as, how, just as; (Conj.) in order that

πᾶς, πασα, πᾶν: all, every, each, whole

πειράω (ῶ): to try, attempt, endeavor (+Gen.)

-περ: (Enclitic particle; added to end of a word) Untranslatable but adds force and emphasis

ποιέω (-ῶ): make, do, act, produce, cause

πρόσθεν: (of Time) before, formerly; (Adv. of Space/Place) before, outside, in front of

πρῶτος, -η, -ον: first

τοιοῦτος, τοιαύτη, τοιοῦτο: this sort or kind; this sort of

ὅδε, ἥδε, τόδε: (Demon.) this

φράζω: to show, point out, make known, explain, declare, tell, indicate

φύσις, φύσεως, ἡ: nature, origin, birth

1.1 ἐόντος: Gen. sg. of ἐών, the Ionic pres. part. of εἰμί

τοῦ...λόγος τοῦδ' ἐόντος: Gen. Abs. *With this λόγος being...*

καὶ πρόσθεν...καὶ: *both before....and (after)*

1.2 ἀκούσαντες τὸ πρῶτον: Circum. Participial; *after having heard the first (time)*

γινομένων...πάντων: Gen. Abs. *with all things becoming/coming to be*

1.3 ἐοίκασι: 3ʳᵈ Perf. Pl. Act.; (+ Dat.) ἀπείροισιν; personal use of ἔοικα takes Dat. Part.[ix]

1.4 διαιρέων...φράζων: Pres. Nom. Sg. Act. Part.

ὄκως: Ionic form of ὅπως; *how*

ἐπέων: Ionic form of ἐπῶν; Gen. Pl. of ἔπος

διηγεῦμαι: 1ˢᵗ Sg. Pres. Contr. form of διηγέομαι

ὄκως ἔχει: translate intransitive ἔχω as verb of being; *how it is*

1.5 ὀκόσα: Ionic form of ὁπόσα

ἐγερθέντες: Aor. Nom. Pl. Pass. Participle of ἐγείρω

εὔδοντες: Pres. Nom. Pl. Circum. Participle of εὔδω

ὀκόσα ἐγερθέντες ποιοῦσιν λανθάνει: *whatever they did when they were awake escapes (their) notice*

ὀκόσα εὔδοντες: *whatever they did when sleeping*

Note:

- **1.1**: In Book 3 §5 of his *Rhetoric*, Aristotle reported on the ambiguity inherent to the ἀεὶ, specifically whether it modifies the preceding δὲ λόγου τοῦδ' ἐόντος or the subsequent ἀξύνετοι γίνονται ἄνθρωποι.

- Some translators have sought to preserve this ἀεὶ in both instances with the ἀεὶ occurring in both instances within their translation (See Robinson's Translation).

B 2 διὸ δεῖ ἕπεσθαι τῶι [ξυνῷ, τουτέστι τῷ] κοινῷˑ ξυνὸς γὰρ ὁ κοινός. τοῦ λόγου δ' ἐόντος ξυνοῦ ζώουσιν οἱ πολλοὶ ὡς ἰδίαν ἔχοντες φρόνησιν.

γὰρ: (Conj.) for, since

δεῖ: (w/Acc. or Infin.) it is necessary, it is needful for one to do, one must

διὸ: (Conj.) wherefore, on which account

ἕπομαι: to follow, come after, pursue, obey, submit, understand

ἔχω: to have, hold

ζάω (-ῶ): to live

ἴδιος, -α, -ον: private, personal, one's own, private interests, separate, distinct, peculiar

κοινός, -ή, -όν: common, public, ordinary

λόγος, -ου, ὁ: best to leave it as λόγος (or) as word, account, reason, understanding

πολύς, πολλή, πολύ: (with nouns of mass/amount) a lot of, much, great amount; many

φρόνησις, -εως, ἡ: practical wisdom, thought

ὡς: (as an Adv.) as, just as, so, thus, when

ἕπεσθαι: Pres. Mid. Inf. of ἕπομαι with δεῖ; *one ought to follow* (+Dat.)

ξυνός, -ή, -όν: Ionic form of κοινός, -ή, -όν

τουτέστι: Crasis of τοῦτ' ἔστι

τοῦ...ξυνοῦ: Gen. Sg. Abs.; *with the λόγος being common*

ὁι πολλοὶ: Subject of ζώουσιν; *the many/ the majority (of people)*

ζώουσιν: Ionic/Epic form for the 3rd Pl. Pres. of the Attic ζάω (-ῶ); *they live*

ὡς...ἔχοντες: *as though having*

Note:

- Kirk, Raven, and Schofield contend that ξυνὸς γὰρ ὁ κοινός was an insertion as a gloss by a previous commentator to clarify that ξυνός word is the same as κοινός, albeit in a different dialect.[x]

B 3 (περὶ μεγέθους ἡλίου) εὖρος ποδὸς ἀνθρωπείου.

ἀνθρώπειος, -α, -ον: of or belonging to a human, human

Εὖρος, -ους, τό: width, breath

ἡλίος, - ου ὁ: the sun

μέγεθος, -εος Ionic for μέγαθος, -ους, τό: greatness, magnitude, size, height, stature,

περί: (+ Gen.) concerning or about

πούς, ποδός, ὁ: a foot

περὶ μεγέθους ἡλίου: (Prep. + Gen.) *Concerning the width of the sun*

εὖρος ποδὸς ἀνθρωπείου: (Add ἐστίν here): *(it is the) size of a human foot*

B 4 Si felicitas esset in delectationibus corporis, boves felices diceremus, cum inveniant orobum ad comedendum.

---

bōs, bovis, m. or f.: cow, bull, ox; (Pl.) cattle

comedo, comedere, comedi, comesum: to eat, chew up, consume, devour

corpus, corporis, n.: body

dēlectātiō, dēlectātiōnis, f.: delight, pleasure, amusement

dīcō, dīcere, dīxī, dictum: to say, utter, talk, speak, declare, state, tell, appoint

fēlīcitās, -tātis, f.: happiness, felicity

fēlīx, fēlīcis, m., f., or n.: happy, lucky, blessed, fortunate, fruitful

in: (+Abl.) in, on, upon, among

inveniō, invenīre, invenīvī, inventum: to find, discover, come upon, invent, devise

orobus, ī, m: bitter vetch; a plant used as food for livestock

si: (Conj.) if, supposing that

Si felicitas esset...diceremus: Present Contrary-to-Fact Condition (Imp. Subj. in Protasis and Imp. Subj. in Apodosis).

esset: 3rd Sg. Imp. Act. Subj. of sum (sum, esse, fui, futurus): *was*

diceremus: 1st Pl. Imp. Act. Subj. of dīcō; *we would call*

cum: (+Subj.) Cum Circum. Clause: *when….*

ad comedendum: (ad + Gerundive Expresses Purpose); *for the purposes of consumption* or *for consumption*

B 5

1 καθαίρονται δ' ἄλλως αἵματι μιαινόμενοι οἷον εἴ τις εἰς πηλὸν ἐμβὰς πηλῶι
2 ἀπονίζοιτο. μαίνεσθαι δ' ἂν δοκοίη, εἴ τις αὐτὸν ἀνθρώπων ἐπιφράσαιτο οὕτω
3 ποιέοντα. καὶ τοῖς ἀγάλμασι δὲ τουτέοισιν εὔχονται ὁκοῖον εἴ τις δόμοισι λεσχηνεύοιτο
4 <οὔ τι γινώσκων θεοὺς οὐδ' ἥρωας οἵτινές εἰσι>.

ἄγαλμα, -ατος, τό: image, sign; statue of a god; object of worship; gift
αἱμάς, -άδος, ἡ: blood, stream of blood
ἄλλως: (Adv.) otherwise, differently, generally
ἄν: Used in conditionals; marks an indefinite; (w/ no Protasis) expresses what might have occurred in the past)
ἄνθρωπος,-ου, ὁ: man, human, person
ἀπονίζω: to wash clean, wash off,
αὐτός, -ή, -όν: reflexive; (Art. + form of αὐτός, -ή, -όν) the same
γιγνώσκω: to know, perceive, understand, be aware of
δέ: (Ptcl.) but, but on the other hand, or just leave untranslated
δοκέω (-ῶ): to seem; to think, suppose, imagine, expect
δόμος, -ου, ὁ: house, dwelling
εἰ: (Conj.) if
εἰς: (Prep + Acc.) into, onto, up to, until
ἐμβαίνω: to step in, go on, enter
ἐπιφράζω: to notice, think to do, contrive

εὔχομαι: to pray, long for, wish for, promise, vow
ἥρως, ἥρωος, ὁ/ἡ: hero
θεός, οῦ, ὁ: god, deity
καθαλιρω: to purify, cleanse, wash, purge
καί: (Conj.) and, even, also
λεσχηνεύω: to chat, converse with
μαίνομαι: to rage, be furious, be mad, riot
μιαίνω: to corrupt, taint, defile, stain, sully
οἷος, οἵα, οἷον: just as, as; such as
ὅστις, ἥτις, ὅτι: whoever, anyone, anything which, whichsoever, whatsoever, anything
ὁκοῖος, -α, -ον: of what sort, of whatever kind, of what quality,
οὐ: (Ptcl.) not, non
οὐδέ: (Conj.) and not, nor, but not
οὗτος, αὕτη, τοῦτο: this; (Pl.) those, these
οὕτω: (Adv.) in this way, so
πηλὸς, -οῦ, ὁ/ἡ: mud, clay, earth
ποιέω (-ῶ): make, do, act, produce, cause
τις, τις, τι, (Gen.: τινος): anyone, anything, someone, something

1 καθαίρονται: 3rd Pl. Pres. Mid Ind.; *they purify themselves*
αἵματι: Dat. of Means[xi]; *with blood*
ἐμβὰς: Aor. Act. Sg. Part. of ἐμβαίνω
οἷον εἴ τις: *just as if someone*
πηλῶι: Dat. of Means[xii]; *with mud*
2 ἀπονίζοιτο: 3rd Sg. Pres. Mid./Pass. Opt.; *would wash themselves*
ἂν δοκοίη...εἴ τις...ἐπιφράσαιτο; FLV Conditional; *would...should*
μαίνεσθαι δ' ἂν δοκοίη: δοκοίη 3rd Sg. Pres. Act. Opt.; *he (antecedent τις) would seem to be mad* (μαίνεσθαι is Pres. Mid./Pas. Inf.)
τις αὐτὸν ἀνθρώπων...ἐπιφράσαιτο οὕτω ποιέοντα: ἐπιφράσαιτο is 3rd Sg. Aor. Opt. Mid.; *any among men would notice him doing so*
3 τοῖς ἀγάλμασι δὲ...εὔχονται: *they pray to these very statues/signs*
ὁκοῖον: Adverbial; *as/just as*
λεσχηνεύοιτο: 3rd Pres. Opt. Mid./Pas. of λεσχηνεύω
4 τι: Adverbial Accusative[xiii]; *in any manner*

18

B 6 ὁ ἥλιος οὐ μόνον, καθάπερ ὁ Ἡ. φησι, νέος ἐφ' ἡμέρηι ἐστίν, ἀλλ' ἀεὶ νέος συνεχῶς.

ἐπί: (+ Dat.) on, upon, in
ἐστίν: 3rd present of εἰμί; he/she/it is
ἥλιος, - ου ὁ: sun
ἡμέρα, -ας, ἡ: day; particular day; each day
καθάπερ: (Adv.) exactly as

μόνος, -η, ον: alone, one, unique
νέος, -η, -ον: new, young, fresh, youthful
οὐ: (Particle) not, non
συνεχής, -ές: contiguous, continuous, unremitting, constant

οὐ μόνον: (Adv. of μόνος) *not only*
ἐφ': elided form of prep. ἐπί
ἡμέρηι: Ionic form of ἡμέρα; *on each day*
συνεχῶς: (Adv.) continuously, continually, unceasingly

B 7 εἰ πάντα τὰ ὄντα καπνὸς γένοιτο, ῥῖνες ἂν διαγνοῖεν.

γίγνομαι: become, come into being, be born, be produced
διαγιγνώσκω: to distinguish, discern, determine, know one from the other
εἰ: if

καπνός, καπνοῦ, ὁ: smoke
ὁ, ἡ, τό: the, that
πᾶς, πασα, πᾶν: all, every, each, whole
ῥίς, ῥινός, ἡ: nose, nostrils, (or pipes/conduits)
ὤν, ὄντος: Pres. Part. of εἰμί

εἰ...καπνὸς γένοιτο: Protasis of FLV; *should...would*
πάντα τὰ ὄντα: subject of γένοιτο (Note: neuter plural subjects in Greek take singular verbs] ; *all beings*
γένοιτο: 3rd Sg. Aor. Mid. Opt. of γίγνομαι
ἂν διαγνοῖεν: Apodosis of FLV: *would distinguish*
ῥῖνες: Nom. Pl.; *nostrils*

Β 8 Ἡ. τὸ ἀντίξουν συμφέρον καὶ ἐκ τῶν διαφερόντων καλλίστην ἁρμονίαν [καὶ πάντα κατ' ἔριν γίνεσθαι]

αντίξοος, -ον (ξοῦς, οῦν): opposed, adverse; τὸ ἀντίξοον: opposition

ἁρμονία, -ἡ: joining, harmony, agreement, order

διαφέρω: differ, struggle, quarrel, to be at variance, to carry in different directions or ways

ἐκ: (Prep. + Gen.) out of, from, forth from

ἔρις, -ιδος, ἡ: strife, quarrel, debate, contention, battle, fight, contest, disputation

καί: (Conj.) and, even, also

καλός, -ή, όν: (Adj.) good, beautiful, beauteous, fair, noble,

κατά: (+Acc.) according to, corresponding with, after the fashion of

συμφέρω: is in harmony with, harmonize, occur, unite, gather, collect

Ἡ. (φησί): Implied φησί; *Heraclitus says that (+IS)*
συμφέρον: Pres. Acc. Sg. N/M Part. of συμφέρω
τὸ ἀντίξουν συμφέρον: *the opposite harmonizes*
διαφερόντων: Pres. Gen. Pl. Attrib. Part. of διαφέρω
καλλίστην: Acc. Fem. Sg. Superl. of καλός
καὶ πάντα... γίνεσθαι: *and all things become/happen/come to be*

Β 9 ὄνους σύρματ' ἂν ἑλέσθαι μᾶλλον ἢ χρυσόν·

αἱρέω: choose, select, prefer

ὄνος, -ου, ὁ and ἡ: ass or donkey

σύρμα, -ατος, τό: refuse, trash, sweepings

ἄν: (Particle) used to indicate limitation or mode

μᾶλλον: (Comp.) (Adv.) more, more strongly

ἢ: (with Comp.) than

χρυσός, -οῦ, ὁ: gold coin, gold

[**Η. (φησί)**] **ὄνους...ἑλέσθαι**: IS; *[Heraclitus says that] donkeys...*
ἂν ἑλέσθαι: Aor. Mid. Inf. of αἱρέω with ἄν; translates like an ordinary Aor. Ind. verb;[xiv] *preferred*

B 10 συλλάψιες· ὅλα καὶ οὐχ ὅλα, συμφερόμενον διαφερόμενον, συνᾷδον διᾷδον καὶ ἐκ πάντων ἓν καὶ ἐξ ἑνὸς πάντα.

διαείδω: to be dissonant
διαφέρω: to be drawn apart, to be disrupted,
εἷς, μία, ἕν: (Gen. ἑνός) one
ἐκ: (Prep. + Gen.) out of, from, forth from
καί: (Conj.) and, even, also
ὅλος, -η, -ον: whole, entire, utter, complete in all its parts

οὐκ: (Particle) not, no
πᾶς, πᾶσα, πᾶν: all, every, each
σύλληψις, -εως, ἡ: conjunctions, inclusion, taking together, comprehension, conception
συμφέρω: to come together, collect, bring together, gathering
συνᾴδω: to be in accord with, agree with

συλλάψιες: Ionic Nom. Pl. of σύλληψις; *couples* OR *pairings*
ἐξ: Alt. form of ἐκ that occurs before word beginning with a vowel
συμφερόμενον διαφερόμενον: Pres. Sg. Neut. Act. Parts. modifies ἕν
διᾷδον συνᾷδον: Pres. Sg. Neut. Act. Parts. modifies ἕν
καί...καί: *both...and*

B 11 πᾶν γὰρ ἑρπετὸν πληγῆι νέμεται, ὥς φησιν Ἡράκλειτος.

γάρ: (Conj.) for, since
ἑρπετόν, -οῦ, τό: animal, quadruped, reptile, living being
Ἡράκλειτος: Heraclitus
νέμω: to drive to pasture, tend, pasture

πᾶς, πᾶσα, πᾶν: all, every, each
πληγή, -ῆς, ἡ: stroke, blow, physical strike
φημί: to say, speak, agree
ὡς: (Adv.) as, just as, like

πληγῆι: Dat. Sg. of πληγή; Dat. of Instrument; *with a blow/strike*
νέμεται: 3rd Sg. Pres. Mid./Pas. Ind. of νέμω; takes πᾶν... ἑρπετὸν as sub.

B 12 ποταμοῖσι τοῖσιν αὐτοῖσιν ἐμβαίνουσιν ἕτερα καὶ ἕτερα ὕδατα ἐπιρρεῖ.

αὐτός, -ή, -όν: (Reflexive Pro.) himself, herself, itself; (Art. + αὐτός, -ή, -όν) the same
ἐμβαίνω: to step in, go on, step upon, embark
ἐπιρρέω: flow upon, keep flowing, streaming on

ἕτερος, -α, -ον: other, different, another
καί: (Conj.) and, even, also
ποταμός, -οῦ, ὁ: river, stream
ὕδωρ, ὕδατος, τό: water

    τοῖσιν: Dat. Pl. M. Art.
    ἐμβαίνουσιν: Pres. Dat. Pl. Act. Part. of ἐμβαίνω
    ποταμοῖσι τοῖσιν αὐτοῖσιν ἐμβαίνουσιν: *to those stepping in the same rivers*
    ἕτερα καὶ ἕτερα ὕδατα ἐπιρρεῖ: N. Pl. Sub. can take a Sg. Verb; *different and other waters*

B 13 δεῖ γὰρ τὸν χαρίεντα μήτε ῥυπᾶν μήτε αὐχμεῖν μήτε βορβόρωι χαίρειν καθ᾽ Ἡράκλειτον. ὕες βορβόρωι ἥδονται μᾶλλον ἢ καθαρῶι ὕδατι.

αὐχμέω (ῶ): to be squalid, to be unwashed
βόρβορος, -ου, ὁ: filth, mire
δεῖ: (w/Acc. or Infin.) it is necessary, it is needful for one to do, one must
ἥδομαι: to enjoy oneself; to be glad; to delight in; to be amused; to be pleased;
καθαρός, ά, όν: clean, pure, unmixed, clear
κατά: (+Acc.) according to, corresponding with, after the fashion of

μάλα: (Adv.) much, very, exceedingly; (Comp μᾶλλον) more
μήτε...μήτε: (Correl.) neither...nor
ῥυπάω (ῶ): to be filthy
ὕδωρ, ὕδατος, τό: water
ὖς, ὑός, ὁ or ἡ: pig, swine, hog
χαίρω: to rejoice, to be glad, take pleasure in, delight in

    ῥυπᾶν: Pres. Act. Inf. of Contract Verb ῥυπάω
    μᾶλλον ἢ: (Comp. + ἢ) *more than*
    ὕες: Nom. Pl. of ὖς
    βορβόρωι ἥδονται: (Verb + Dat.); *take pleasure in filth*
    καθαρῶι ὕδατι: *in clean water*

B 14 τίσι δὴ μαντεύεται Ἡ. ὁ Ἐφέσιος; νυκτιπόλοις, μάγοις, βάκχοις, λήναις, μύσταις· τούτοις ἀπειλεῖ τὰ μετὰ θάνατον, τούτοις μαντεύεται τὸ πῦρ· τὰ γὰρ νομιζόμενα κατ' ἀνθρώπους μυστήρια ἀνιερωστὶ μυεῦνται.

ἄνθρωπος,-ου, ὁ: man, human, person
ἀνίερος, -η, -ον: impious, unholy, profane, sacrilegious
ἀπειλέω (ῶ): to threaten
βάκχάω: to be in Bacchant frenzy, rave
γάρ: (Conj.) for, since
Ἐφέσιος, -α, -ον: Ephesian, native of Ephesus
θάνατος, -ου, ὁ: death
κατά: (Prep. +Acc.) in, along, through, downwards, according to
Λῆναι, αἱ: The Bacchanals
Μάγος, -ου, ὁ: Magi, one of the priests of Persia; OR, enchanter, wizard, imposter, charlatan

μαντεύομαι: to divine, prophesy, forbode, presage, surmise, draw divinations, consult an oracle, seek divinations
μετά: (Prep. +Acc.) after, into the middle of, among, in pursuit of, between, afterwards
μυέω (ῶ): to initiate or be initiated into the mysteries.
μυστήριον, -ου, τό: mysteries, referring to the Dionysian Mysteries or rites
μύστης, -ου, ὁ: an initiate
νομίζω: to believe, think, esteem, acknowledge
νυκτιπόλος, -ον, -η: roaming at night
πῦρ, πυρός, τό: fire; funeral-fire, sacrificial fire, hearth fire

τίσι: *to/for (those) people*
νυκτιπόλοις... μύσταις: *(to/for) the night-roamers...*
τούτοις ἀπειλεῖ τά: *to these (people) does (Heraclitus) threaten*
τὸ πῦρ: Acc. Obj. of μαντεύεται
τὰ...νομιζόμενα...μυστήρια: *the believed/acknowledged mysteries*
ἀνιερωστὶ: Adv. form of ἀνίερος; *impiously*
μυεῦνται: 3rd Pl. Pres. Mid./Pas. Ind. Cont. Form of μυέω

- For additional information on the Dionysian Cults, Rice and Stambaugh have an excellent brief chapter from *Sources for the Study of Greek Religion* available online, which helps provide additional insight on this fragment.

B 15 εἰ μὴ γὰρ Διονύσωι πομπὴν ἐποιοῦντο καὶ ὕμνεον ᾆσμα αἰδοίοισιν, ἀναιδέστατα εἴργαστ' ἄν· ωὑτὸς δὲ Ἀίδης καὶ Διόνυσος, ὅτεωι μαίνονται καὶ ληναίζουσιν.

Ἀίδης: Hades, god of the underworld, or the underworld itself

αἰδοῖον, -ίου, τό: genitals (whether male or female)

ᾆσμα, -ατος, τό: song, ode, hymn

ἄν: Used in conditionals; marks an indefinite; (w/ no Protasis) expresses what might have occurred in the past

ἀναιδής, -ές: shameless, ruthless

αὐτός, -ή, -όν: reflexive; (Art. + form of αὐτός, -ή, -όν) the same

Διόνυσος, -ου, ὁ: Dionysus, god of revelry and wine

εἰ: (Conj.) if

ἐργάζομαι: to work at, labor, make

ποιέω (-ῶ): make, do, act, produce, cause

καί: (Conj.) and, even, also

ληναίζω: to celebrate Bacchanalian rites

μαίνομαι: to rage, be furious, be mad, riot

μή: (Particle) no, not

ὅστις, ἥτις, ὅτι: whoever, anyone, anything

πομπή, -ῆς, ἡ: solemn procession, parade, escort

ὑμνέω: to sing, praise in sing, hymn

εἰ μὴ...ἐποιοῦντο: 3rd Pl. Mid. Imp. of ποιέω; *if they (themselves) were not making*

Διονύσωι: Ionic Dat. Sg.; *for Dionysus*

ὕμνεον: 3rd Imp. Pl. Act. of ὑμνέω; *singing*

ᾆσμα αἰδοίοισιν: *hymn to genitals*

ἀναιδέστατα: N. Pl. Superl. Adv. (Superl. Adv. and N. Superl. Adj. are the same form)

εἴργαστ': Elided form of εἴργασται, 3rd Sg. Mid./Pas. Perf. of ἐργάζομαι

ἀναιδέστατα εἴργαστ' ἄν: Unreal Indicative with ἄν[xv]; *it would have been done most shamelessly*

ωὑτὸς: Crasis ὁ + αὐτός

ωὑτὸς δὲ Ἀίδης καὶ Διόνυσος: *Hades and Dionysus are the same*

ὅτεωι: Ionic Dat. Sg. of ὅστις; *for whom*

B 16 τὸ μὴ δῦνόν ποτε πῶς ἄν τις λάθοι;

δύω: to sink, plunge, set
λανθάνω: to escape notice, escape, pass over
μή: not
πότε: (Interrogative Particle) ever, at any time, when

πῶς: How? (With particles like ἄν or κε, used with the optative)
τις, τις, τι, (Gen.: τινος): anyone, anything, someone, something

> **πῶς ἄν τις λάθοι**: Potential Opt. with ἄν;[xvi] *how would one escape*
> **δῦνόν**: Pres. Sg. Act. N. Attrib. Part. of δύω; obj. of λάθοι
> **τὸ μὴ δῦνόν**: *a thing (that) does not set/sink*

B 17 οὐ γὰρ φρονέουσι τοιαῦτα πολλοί, ὁκόσοι ἐγκυρεῦσιν, οὐδὲ μαθόντες γινώσκουσιν, ἑωυτοῖσι δὲ δοκέουσι.

γάρ: (Conj.) for, since
γιγνώσκω: to know, perceive, understand, be aware of
δέ: (Particle) but, but on the other hand, or just leave untranslated
δοκέω (-ῶ): to seem; to think, suppose, imagine, expect
ἑαυτοῦ, -ῆς, -οῦ: No Nom. Sg. reflexive in Attic or Ionic Greek; himself, herself, itself; (Pl.) themselves
ἐγκύρω: to encounter, fall in with, meet with, light upon

μανθάνω: to learn
ὁπόσος, -η, -ο: as many as, however many, how great
οὐ: (Particle) not
οὐδέ: (Conj.) and not, nor, but not,
τοιοῦτος, τοιαύτη, τοιοῦτο: this sort or kind; this sort of πολλοί
φρονέω (ῶ): to think, to have understanding, be wise, be prudent

> **ὁκόσοι**: Ionic Nom. Pl. Masc. of ὁπόσος
> **ἐγκυρεῦσιν**: 3rd Pl. Pres. Act. form of ἐγκύρω
> **μαθόντες**: Aor. Participle; *having learned*
> **γινώσκουσιν**: 3rd Pl. Pres. Act. form of γιγνώσκω
> **ἑωυτοῖσι**: Ionic Dat. Pl. Masc./Neut. of ἑαυτοῦ; *to/for themselves*

B 18 ἐὰν μὴ ἔλπηται, ἀνέλπιστον οὐκ ἐξευρήσει, ἀνεξερεύνητον ἐὸν καὶ ἄπορον.

ἀνέλπιστος, -ον: unhoped for, hopeless, unexpected

ἀνεξερεύνητος, -ον: not to be searched out, unsearched, uninvestigated

ἄπορους, -ον: without passage, impassable, having no way in, hard to discover, hard to solve

ἐάν: if (+Subj.) (+FMV or +PGC)

ἔλπω: to hope, expect, cause to hope, deem, suppose

ἐξευρίσκω: find out, discover, invent, search out, search after, procure

ὤν, οὖσα, ὄν: Present Part. of εἰμί: being, existing, is

ἔλπηται: 3rd Sg. Mid./Pas. Pres. Subj. of ἔλπω

ἐών, ἐοῦσα, ἐόν: Epic/Ionic form of ὤν; present participle of εἰμί

ἔλπηται... ἐξευρήσει: FMV; translate as indicatives

ἀνεξερεύνητον ἐὸν καὶ ἄπορον: Accusative Absolute[xvii]; *since it is not able to be searched and without passage*

B 19 ἀκοῦσαι οὐκ ἐπιστάμενοι οὐδ᾽ εἰπεῖν.

ἀκούω: to hear something (Acc.); to hear from/of someone (+Gen.)

εἶπον: (Aor. 1st. Sg. Ind.) to say, speak

ἐπίσταμαι: to know; know how to do, be able to, capable to do

οὐδὲ: (Conj.) and not, not yet, but not, nor

οὐκ: (Particle) not, no

ἀκοῦσαι...εἰπεῖν: Aor. Act. Inf. of ακουεω and εἶπον

οὐκ ἐπιστάμενοι: Pl. Pres. Act. Part. of ἐπίσταμαι: *(they) do not know how to*[xviii]

οὐδ᾽ εἰπεῖν: *nor (how to) speak*

B 20 Ἡ. γοῦν κακίζων φαίνεται τὴν γένεσιν, ἐπειδὰν φῇ· γενόμενοι ζώειν ἐθέλουσι μόρους τ' ἔχειν, μᾶλλον δὲ ἀναπαύεσθαι, καὶ παῖδας καταλείπουσι μόρους γενέσθαι.

ἀναπαύω: (Mid./Pass.) to take rest; take one's sleep

γένεσις, -εως, ἡ: birth, origin, beginning, genesis

γίγνομαι: to become; to be born; to come to be

γοῦν: Compound Particle of γε οὖν; at least then, at all events

ἐθέλω: to will to, want to, wish to (+Inf.)

ἐπειδὰν: whenever (+Subj.)

ἔχω: to have, hold

ζάω (-ῶ): to live

καί: (Conj.) and, even, also

κακίζω: to abuse, reproach

καταλείπω: to leave behind, forsake, abandon, leave alone

μᾶλλον: (Comp.) (Adv.) more, more strongly

μόρος, -ου, ὁ: fate, destiny

παῖς, παιδός, ὁ/ἡ: child, kid, son, daughter, boy, girl

φαίνω: (+ pred. adj.) appear, come into being, bring to light, shows, displays

φημί: to say, speak, agree

φῇ: 3rd Sg. Subj. Act. of φημί
γενόμενοι: Aor. Mid. Part. of γίγνομαι
ἀναπαύεσθαι: Pres. Mid./Pass. Inf. of ἀναπαύω
παῖδας καταλείπουσι μόρους γενέσθαι: *they leave behind children that come to (have their own) fates*
γενέσθαι: Pres. Mid./Pass. Inf. of γίγνομαι

B 21 θάνατός ἐστιν ὁκόσα ἐγερθέντες ὁρέομεν, ὁκόσα δὲ εὕδοντες ὕπνος.

ἐγείρω: to awaken, rouse, stir

εὕδω: to sleep

θάνατος, -ου, ὁ: death

ὁπόσος, -η, -ον: as many as, as much as; (In Indirect Questions) however much, however many

ὁράω (ῶ): to see

ὕπνος, -ου, ὁ: sleep, rest, slumber

ὁκόσα: Neut. Pl. Ionic of ὁπόσος
ἐγερθέντες: Masc. Nom. Pass. Aor. Part. of ἐγείρω
ὁρέομεν: 1st Pl. Pres. Act. of ὁράω
εὕδοντες: Pl. Pres. Act. Part. of εὕδω

B 22 χρυσὸν γὰρ οἱ διζήμενοι γῆν πολλὴν ὀρύσσουσι καὶ εὑρίσκουσιν ὀλίγον.

γάρ: (Conj.) for, since
γῆ, γῆς, ἡ: earth, soil, land
δίζημαι: to seek out, look for, desire
εὑρίσκω: to find, discover, happen upon by
chance, acquire, obtain, fetch

ὀλίγος, -η, -ον: few, little, low
ὀρύσσω: to dig
πολύς, πολλή, πολύ: (with nouns of
mass/amount) a lot of, much, great amount; (pl.)
many
χρυσός, οὖ, ὁ: gold

   οἱ διζήμενοι: Attrib. Part.; *the ones seeking for* (Sub. of ὀρύσσουσι and εὑρίσκουσιν)
   χρυσόν: Obj. of διζήμενοι
   ὀλίγον: Obj. of ὀρύσσουσι and εὑρίσκουσιν

B 23 Δίκης ὄνομα οὐκ ἂν ᾔδεσαν, εἰ ταῦτα μὴ ἦν.

δίκη, -ας, ἡ: justice, right, order, custom
εἰ: (conj.) if
μὴ: (Particle) no, not
οἶδα: (Perf. translated as Pres.); *I know*

ὄνομα, ὀνόματος, τό: by name, name
οὐκ: (Particle) not, no
οὗτος, αὕτη, τοῦτο: this; (Pl.) those, these

   οὐκ ἂν ᾔδεσαν: 3rd Pl. Plup. of οἶδα: *they would not have known*
   εἰ...ἦν: Protasis of Past CTF, a conditional which expresses unreality
   εἰ ταῦτα μὴ ἦν: N. Pl. can be subjects of Sg. Verbs; *if these things were not*

B 24 ἀρηιφάτους θεοὶ τιμῶσι καὶ ἄνθρωποι.

ἀρείφατος, -ον: slain by Ares, slain in war
θεός, οὖ, ὁ: god, deity

τιμάω (-ῶ): honor, hold in honor, revere, treat
honorably, pay honorably

   ἀρηιφάτους: Acc. Pl.; *slain by Ares, slain in war*
   τιμῶσι: 3rd Pl. Pres. Act. Ind. of τιμάω

B 25 μόροι γὰρ μέζονες μέζονας μοίρας λαγχάνουσι.

λαγχάνω: to obtain, to obtain by lot, obtain as one's portion
μέγας, μεγάλη, μέγα: big, great, vast, mighty, strong, important

μοῖρα, -ας, ἡ: part, portion, division, degree, share; destiny, lot
μόρος, -ου, ὁ: fate, destiny

μέζονες/μέζονας: Ionic comp. Adj. forms for Nom. and Acc. Pl. (respectively) of μέγας, μεγάλη, μέγα
λαγχάνουσι: 3rd Pl. Pres. Act. of λαγχάνω

B 26 ἄνθρωπος ἐν εὐφρόνηι φάος ἅπτεται ἑαυτῶι ἀποθανὼν, ἀποσβεσθεὶς [ὄψεις], ζῶν δὲ ἅπτεται τεθνεῶτος εὕδων, ἀποσβεσθεὶς ὄψεις, ἐγρηγορὼς ἅπτεται εὕδοντος.

ἄνθρωπος, -ου, ὁ: man, human, person
ἀποθνήσκω: to die
ἀποσβέννυμι: to extinguish, quench, go out, vanish, cease, extinguish
ἅπτω: to kindle, set on fire
ἑαυτοῦ, -ῆς, -οῦ: (No Nom.) himself, herself, itself
ἐγείρω: to awaken, rouse, stir
ἐν: (Prep. + Dat.) in, on, at, among

εὕδω: to sleep
εὐφρόνη, -ης, ἡ: night (Lit: the kindly/good time)
ζάω (-ῶ): to live
θνήσκω: to die, to be dying
ὄψις, -εως, ἡ: sight, view, appearance, face, vision, act of seeing, looking
φάος, -εος, τό: light, daylight, day

φάος ἅπτεται: 3rd Sg. Mid. Pres.; *sets a light/fire for oneself*
ἀποθανὼν: Aor. Sg. Circum. Part. of ἀποθνήσκω; *since it extinguished*
ἀποσβεσθεὶς: Part. Sg. Aor. M. Nom. of ἀποσβέννυμι; *having extinguished*
τεθνεῶτος: Part. Sg. Perf. Act. M. Gen. of θνήσκω; Mini Circum. Gen. Abs. of Concession[xix]: *sleeping, although he/she/it has died*
ἐγρηγορὼς: Perf. Act. Part. of ἐγείρω
εὕδοντος: Circum. Gen. Abs. of Concession like τεθνεῶτος

B 27 ἀνθρώπους μένει ἀποθανόντας ἄσσα οὐκ ἔλπονται οὐδὲ δοκέουσιν.

ἄνθρωπος,-ου, ὁ: man, human, person
ἀποθνήσκω: to die
δοκέω (-ῶ): to seem; to think, suppose, imagine, expect
ἔλπω: to hope, expect, cause to hope
μένω: to stay, remain; wait, await, expect (+Acc or Inf.)

ὅστις, ἥτις, ὅτι: whoever, anyone, anything which, whichsoever, whatsoever, anything, he/she who, it which
οὐδὲ: (Conj.) and not, not yet, but not, nor
οὐκ: (Particle) no, not

> **μένει**: 3rd Sg. Pres. Act.; take here impersonally as *there await/waits* +Acc. ἀνθρώπους... ἀποθανόντας
> **ἀποθανόντας**: Aor. Acc. Pl. Part. of ἀποθνήσκω; matches ἄνθρωπος
> **ἄσσα**: Epic N. Pl. Acc. of ὅστις, ἥτις, ὅτι

B 28 δοκέοντα γὰρ ὁ δοκιμώτατος γινώσκει, φυλάσσει· καὶ μέντοι καὶ Δίκη καταλήψεται ψευδῶν τέκτονας καὶ μάρτυρας.

γάρ: (Conjunction) for, since
γιγνώσκω: to know, perceive, understand, be aware of
Δίκη, -ης, ἡ: goddess of justice
δοκέω (-ῶ): to seem; to think, suppose, imagine, expect
δόκιμος, -η, -ον: trustworthy, esteemed, acceptable, noble, excellent
καί: (Conj.) and, even, also

καταλαμβάνω: to seize, lay hold of
μάρτυς, μάρτυρος, ὁ or ἡ: witness
μέντοι: (Particle) however, indeed, to be sure
τέκτων, ονος, ὁ: maker, craftsman, workman, author, master
φυλάσσω: to keep watch and ward, keep guard, watch, defend, guard
ψεῦδος, -εος, τό: lie, falsehood, deceit, fallacy

> **δοκέοντα**: Acc. Pres. Part. Ionic of δοκέω; Obj. of γινώσκει; *what seems (to be the case)*
> **δοκιμώτατος**: Superl. of δόκιμος; *most esteemed*
> **γινώσκει**: Ionic 3rd Sg. Pres. of γίγνωσκω
> **(καὶ) φυλάσσει**: 3rd Sg. Pres. of φυλάσσω; *and keeps watch*
> **καταλήψεται**: 3rd Sg. Fut. of καταλαμβάνω
> **καὶ μέντοι καὶ**: *and however even...*
> **τέκτονας καὶ μάρτυρας**: Acc. Obj. of καταλήψεται

B 29 αἱρεῦνται γὰρ ἓν ἀντὶ ἁπάντων οἱ ἄριστοι, κλέος ἀέναον θνητῶν· οἱ δὲ πολλοὶ κεκόρηνται ὅκωσπερ κτήνεα.

-**περ**: (Enclitic Ptcl.) Untranslatable but adds force and emphasis

ἀέναος, -α, -ον: ever-flowing, everlasting

αἱρέω: (Act.) take, seize, grasp; (Mid.) prefer, select, choose

ἀντί: (Prep. + Gen.) instead of, in the place of, over against, opposite, in return for

ἅπας, ἅπασα, ἅπαν: the whole, all together, everything, any possible thing

ἄριστος, -η, -ον: best, noblest, bravest, most excellent

δέ: (Particle) but on the other hand, but, or just leave untranslated

εἷς, μία, ἕν: one

θνητός, -ή, -όν: mortal, human, mortal creature, one liable to death

κλέος, τό: fame, renown, glory, rumor, report

κορέννυμι: to satiate, fill

κτῆνος, κτήνους, τό: flocks, herds, beast, ox, sheep, horse

ὅπως: (Adv.) in such a manner, as, exactly as

πολύς, πολλή, πολύ: many, majority, all; **οἱ πολλοί**: the many, the majority, the multitude

αἱρεῦνται: Ionic form for the 3rd Mid./Pass. Pres. Pl. of αἱρέω (ῶ)

ἕν: Neut. Acc. of ἕν; obj. of αἱρεῦνται

ἀντὶ ἁπάντων: ἀντὶ (Prep. + Gen.); *instead of all other things*

κλέος ἀέναον θνητῶν: Partitive Gen.[xx]; *immortal glory among mortals*

ὅκως: Ionic form of ὅπως

κεκόρηνται: 3rd pl. Perf. Ind. Mid./Pass.: *have satisfied themselves/ have been satisfied*

31

B 30 κόσμον <τόνδε>, τὸν αὐτὸν ἁπάντων, οὔτε τις θεῶν οὔτε ἀνθρώπων ἐποίησεν, ἀλλ' ἦν ἀεὶ καὶ ἔστιν καὶ ἔσται πῦρ ἀείζωον, ἁπτόμενον μέτρα καὶ ἀποσβεννύμενον μέτρα.

ἀείζωος, -ον: ever-living, everlasting; Compound of ἀεί and ζωός, -ά, -όν
ἀλλά: (Conj.) but
ἄνθρωπος,-ου, ὁ: man, human, person
ἅπας, ἅπασα, ἅπαν: the whole, all together, everything, any possible thing
ἀποσβέννυμι: to extinguish, quench, go out, vanish, cease, extinguish
ἅπτω: to kindle, set on fire
αὐτός, -ή, -όν: reflexive; (Art. + form of αὐτός, -ή, -όν) the same
θεός, -οῦ, ὁ: god, divine, deity

κόσμος, -ου, ὁ: world-order, universe
μέτρον, -ου, τό: measure, rule, length, space, dimension
ὅδε, ἥδε, τόδε: (Demon.) this
οὔτε...οὔτε: (Correl.) neither...nor
ποιέω (-ῶ): make, do, act, produce, cause
πῦρ, πυρός, τό: fire; funeral-fire, sacrificial fire, hearth-fire
τις, τι, (Gen.: τινος): anyone, anything, someone, something

οὔτε τις θεῶν οὔτε ἀνθρώπων: take the two Genitives partitively; *neither anyone of the gods nor of men*
ἔσται: 3rd Sg. Fut. Act. Ind. of εἰμί; πῦρ as subject
ἁπτόμενον...ἀποσβεννύμενον: Sg. Pres. Mid./Pass. Part. of ἅπτω and ἀποσβέννυμι; both have μέτρα as their objects

B 31 πυρὸς τροπαί· πρῶτον θάλασσα, θαλάσσης δὲ τὸ μὲν ἥμισυ γῆ, τὸ δὲ ἥμισυ πρηστήρ......θάλασσα διαχέεται, καὶ μετρέεται εἰς τὸν αὐτὸν λόγον, ὁκοῖος πρόσθεν ἦν ἢ γενέσθαι γῆ.

αὐτός, -ή, -όν: reflexive; (Art. + form of αὐτός, -ή, -όν) the same

γῆ, γῆς, ἡ: earth, soil, land

γίγνομαι: become, come into being, be born, be produced

δέ: (Particle) but on the other hand, but, or just leave untranslated

διαχέω (ῶ): to liquify, melt, fuse

εἰς: (Prep + Acc.) into, onto, up to, until

ἤ: (Conj.) or

ἥμισυς, -υ: half

θάλαττα, -ης, ἡ: sea, sea-water, salt-water

καί: (Conj.) and, even, also

λόγος, -ου, ὁ: best to leave it as λόγος (or) as word, account, reason, understanding

μέν...δέ: on the one hand...on the other hand

μετρέω (ῶ): to measure, count

ὁκοῖος, -α, -ον: of what sort, of whatever kind, of what quality

πρηστήρ, -ῆρος, ὁ: hurricane, water spout

πρόσθεν: (of Time) before, formerly; (Adv. of Space/Place) before, outside, in front of

πρῶτος, -η, -ον: first, foremost, earliest

πῦρ, πυρός, τό: fire; funeral-fire, sacrificial fire, hearthfire

τροπή, -ῆς, ἡ: turn, change

πυρὸς τροπαί·: *the changes of fire*

πρῶτον: (Adv.) *first*

θαλάσσης: Gen. of Source; *from sea*

τὸ μὲν ἥμισυ... τὸ δὲ ἥμισυ: *one half...the other half*

διαχέεται... μετρέεται: Ionic 3rd Sg. Pres. Mid./Pas. forms

ἤ: with IQ ἤ is untranslated and used epexegetically of what's preceding it[xxi]

πρόσθεν ἦν ἢ γενέσθαι γῆ: (literally) *before the earth was to come to be*

33

B 32 ἓν τὸ σοφὸν μοῦνον λέγεσθαι οὐκ ἐθέλει καὶ ἐθέλει Ζηνὸς ὄνομα.

ἐθέλω: to will, want, wish
εἷς, μία, ἓν: one
Ζεύς, Ζηνὸς, ὁ: Zeus
λέγω: say, speak, converse, tell a story

μοῦνον: Ionic form of μόνον; (Adj.) alone;
(Adv..) only, solely
ὄνομα, ὀνόματος, τό: by name, name
οὐκ: (Particle) not, no
σοφὸς, -ή, -όν: wise, prudent, intelligent

ἓν τὸ σοφὸν μοῦνον: Subj. of οὐκ ἐθέλει καὶ ἐθέλει; *only one wise thing*
λέγεσθαι: Pres. Mid./Pass. Inf. of λέγω; *to be called*

B 33 νόμος καὶ βουλῆι πείθεσθαι ἑνός.

βουλή, -ῆς, -ἡ: counsel, determination, advice
εἷς, μία, ἔν: (Gen. ἑνός) one

νόμος, -ου, ὁ: custom, law, ordinance
πείθω: (Act.) persuade, convince; (Mid./Pas.) to
obey, trust, believe (+ Dat.)

νόμος καὶ: (implied + ἐστίν) *it is even a law*
ἑνός: (Gen. of εἷς or ἕν): *of one*
βουλῆι: Dat. Sg. of βουλή; Obj. of πείθεσθαι
πείθεσθαι: Pres. Mid./Pass. Inf. of πείθω

B 34 ἀξύνετοι ἀκούσαντες κωφοῖσιν ἐοίκασι· φάτις αὐτοῖσιν μαρτυρεῖ παρεόντας ἀπεῖναι.

ἀξύνετος, -ον: witless, devoid of understanding, not able to understand

ἀκούω: to hear something (Acc.); to hear from/of someone (+Gen.)

ἄπειμι: to be absent, to be away, to be far from

ἔοικα: (Perf. Act. form translated in a pres. aspect) to seem to, to be like (+Dat.)

κωφός, -ή, -όν: deaf and dumb, mute, dull, obtuse,

μαρτυρέω (ῶ): to bear witness to (+Dat.), give evidence, bear witness

πάρειμι: to be present, to be by, to be near, to be at hand or ready

φάτις, ἡ: saying, proverb, voice from heaven, an oracle

ἀκούσαντες: Pl. Aor. Act. Part. of ἀκούω; Concessive Part.[xxii]; *although they heard*
ἐοίκασι: 3rd Pl. Perf. Ind. Act.; ἀξύνετοι is the Pl. Nom. Subject
αὐτοῖσιν: Dat. of Reference; *to them*
φάτις αὐτοῖσιν μαρτυρεῖ παρεόντας ἀπεῖναι: *the saying bears witness to them:*
(that they are) present (while) being absent

B 35 χρὴ γὰρ εὖ μάλα πολλῶν ἵστορας φιλοσόφους ἄνδρας εἶναι καθ' Ἡράκλειτον.

ἀνήρ, ἀνδρός, ὁ: man

γάρ: (Conjunction) for, since

εὖ: (Adv.) well

ἵστωρ, -ορος, ὁ: wise man, one who knows right, a judge, or knowing

κατά: (Prep. +Acc.) in, along, through, downwards, according to

μάλα: (Adv.) very, exceedingly

πολύς, πολλή, πολύ: (with nouns of mass/amount) a lot of, much, great amount; many

φιλόσοφος, -ου, ὁ: Literally: philosopher; lover of wisdom, one who speculates on truth and reality; or φιλόσοφος, -η, -ον: philosophic

χρή: (Imp. +Inf.) it is necessary, one must, one ought, it must needs

χρὴ... φιλοσόφους ἄνδρας εἶναι: *it is necessary that philosophic men be*
πολλῶν ἵστορας: *knowers of many (subjects)*

B 36 ψυχῆισιν θάνατος ὕδωρ γενέσθαι, ὕδατι δὲ θάνατος γῆν γενέσθαι, ἐκ γῆς δὲ ὕδωρ γίνεται, ἐξ ὕδατος δὲ ψυχή.

γῆ, γῆς, ἡ: earth, soil, land
γίγνομαι: to become; to be born; to come to be
δέ: (Particle) but on the other hand, but, or just leave untranslated

ἐκ: (Prep. + Gen.) out of, from, forth from
θάνατος, -ου, ὁ: death
ὕδωρ, ὕδατος, τό: water
ψυχή, -ῆς, ἡ: spirit, soul, life, ghost

ψυχῆισιν: Ionic Fem. Dat. Pl. of ψυχή: *to/for spirits*
γενέσθαι: Pres. Mid./Pass. Infin. of γίγνομαι; (+ implied ἐστίν) *it is death to become*
δὲ...γῆν: Acc. of Respect; *but with respect to earth*
γίνεται: Ionic of γίγνεται, 3rd Pres. Mid./Pass. of γίγνομαι; take ὕδωρ as its subject

---

B 37 si modo credimus Ephesio Heracleto qui ait sues caeno cohortales aves pulvere vel cinere lavari.

---

aiō, ere: to say, assert,
avis, avis, f.: bird, avian
caenum, -ī, n.: dirt, filth, mire, mud
cinis, cineris, m.: ashes, especially of a corpse
cohortalis, -is, -e: pertaining to swine or a cattle/poultry yard
crēdō, crēdere, crēdidī, crēditum: (+Dat.) to trust, to believe, to have confidence in
Ephesius, -a, -um: of or related to Ephesus (ancient city in Ionia which was Heraclitus' home)

lavō, lavāre, lāvī, lavātum: to wash, bathe, lave
modo: (Adv.) only, even, in any way
pulvis, pulveris, m.: dust
quī, quae, quod: (Rel. Pro.) who, which, that
si: (Conj.) if, supposing that
suus, -a, -um: his/her/its own; (Pl.) their own
vel:(Conj. and Adv.) or, or else

si modo: *if only*
lavari: Pres. Pass. Inf. of lavō
qui ait...lavari: Relative Clause with internal Indirect Statement; *who says that swine are washed*
pulvere vel cinere: Abl. of Means; *birds are washed by (means of) dust or ash*

B 38 δοκεῖ δὲ κατά τινας πρῶτος ἀστρολογῆσαι . . . μαρτυρεῖ δ' αὐτῶι καὶ Ἡ. καὶ Δημόκριτος.

ἀστρολογέω (-ῶ): to study the stars or study astronomy
Δημόκριτος: Pre-Socratic Philosopher and Physicist; famous along with Leucippus as being an Atomist[xxiii]
δοκέω (-ῶ): to seem; to think, suppose, imagine, expect
Ἡ.: Heraclitus

κατά: (+Acc.) according to, corresponding with, after the fashion of
μαρτυρέω (ῶ): bear witness; (with Dat. of Person) bear witness to/confirm that something is the case; (with Inf.) give evidence/testify that something is the case
πρῶτος, -η, -ον: first, foremost, earliest
τις, τι, (Gen.: τινος): anyone, anything, someone, something

> **δοκεῖ**: 3rd Sg. Pres. form of δοκέω (-ῶ); the implied subject is *Thales*, the Pre-Socratic philosopher and astronomer
> **αὐτῶι**: Dat. from μαρτυρεῖ; *to this*
> **καὶ Ἡ. καὶ Δημόκριτος**: *both Heraclitus and Democritus*

B 39 ἐν Πριήνηι Βίας ἐγένετο ὁ Τευτάμεω, οὗ πλείων λόγος ἢ τῶν ἄλλων.

ἄλλος, -η, -ον: another, one besides; (w/Art.) the rest, the others
Βίας, Βίαντος, ὁ: Bias; traditionally considered as one of the Seven Wise Men of Ancient Greece.
γίγνομαι: to become; to be born; to come to be
ἐν: (Prep. + Dat.) in or on

λόγος, -ου, ὁ: best to leave it as λόγος (or) as word, account, reason, understanding
πλείων, πλεῖον: comparative of πολύς, πολλή, πολύ; more, greater
Πριήνη, ἡ: Priene; ancient Greek city in Ionia on the western coast of Turkey

> **ἐγένετο**: 3rd Sg. 2nd Aor; *was born*
> **ὁ Τευτάμεω**: *the son of Teutamos*
> **οὗ**: Gen. Sg. Rel. Pro. (Lit.: of whose or of whom); *whose*
> **πλείων...ἢ**: (+Gen. of Comp.) *greater than*

B 40 πολυμαθίη νόον <ἔχειν> οὐ διδάσκει· Ἡσίοδον γὰρ ἂν ἐδίδαξε καὶ Πυθαγόρην αὖτίς τε Ξενοφάνεά τε καὶ Ἑκαταῖον.

αὖθις: (Adv.) (of time) again, anew; (of place) back, back again; (of future time) hereafter

γὰρ: (Conj.) for, since

διδάσκω: to teach, instruct, train

Ἑκαταῖος, -ου, ὁ: Hecataeus; specifically Hecataeus of Miletus (550 BCE – 476 BCE), a prominent Greek historian and geographer

ἔχω: to have, hold

Ἡσίοδος, -ου, ὁ: Hesiod (~700 BC); one of the two most famous ancient Greek Epic poets; his works included the *Theogony* and *Works and Days*.

νόος, νόου, ὁ: intelligence, intellect, mind, sense, wit, reason, thought

Ξενοφάνης, -ους, ὁ: Xenophanes; specifically Xenophanes of Colophon (570 BCE – 478 BCE), a Pre-Socratic philosopher and travelling teacher.

οὐ: (Particle) not

πολυμαθία, -ας, ἡ: much learning or learning many things (Compound of πολύς, πολλή, πολύ "much" and μανθάνω "to learn")

Πυθαγόρας, -ου, ὁ: Pythagoras; Pythagoras of Samos (the famous pre-Socratic philosopher most renowned for his philosophical and mathematical teachings which would later form the Pythagorean school of philosophy)

πολυμαθίη: Ionic form of πολυμαθία

<ἔχειν>: Likely insertion by later commentator; *πολυμαθίη does not teach one <to have> νόον*

ἂν ἐδίδαξε: ἄν + Ind. Aor. expresses generality, specifically in past time; *it would have taught*

Πυθαγόρην: Acc. Sg. of Attic Πυθαγόρας

αὖτίς: Epic/Ionic form of αὖθις

B 41 εἶναι γὰρ ἓν τὸ σοφόν, ἐπίστασθαι γνώμην, ὁτέη ἐκυβέρνησε πάντα διὰ πάντων.

γάρ: (Conj.) for, since

γνώμη, -ης, ἡ: purpose, intention; motion; judgment, opinion, thought

διά: (Prep. + Gen.) through, throughout, along

εἷς, μία, ἕν: (Gen. ἑνός) one

ἐπίσταμαι: to know, be able, to be assured, observe, understand

κεβερνάω (-ῶ): steer, guide, govern, act as pilot, act as a helmsman

οἷος, οἵα, οἷον: just as, as; such as

ὅπη: (Adv.) wherever, in any direction/manner, by what way

πᾶς, πᾶσα, πᾶν: all, every, each

σοφός, -ή, -όν: wise, prudent, clever, shrewd, learned, universally and ideally wise, ingenious

εἶναι γὰρ ἓν τὸ σοφόν: (Implied Ἡ. φησιν for IS); *(Heraclitus says that) the wise (thing) is one*

ἐπίστασθαι: Pres. Mid./Pas. Inf. of ἐπίσταμαι; *to know the γνώμην*

ὁτέη: see note below

ἐκυβέρνησε: 3rd Sg. Aor. Ind. Act. of κεβερνάω

Notes:

- **ὁτέη** is a textual corruption since it corresponds to no exact form across dialects (even the following ἐκυβέρνησε is disputed from the manuscripts)
    - **Above: Diels-Kranz (1903) & Burnet (1912)**: ὁτέη ἐκυβέρνησε
    - **The following is a brief synopsis of scholarly**
        - **Bywater**: ἥτε οἱ ἐγκυβερνήσει[xxiv]
        - **Bernays**: ἥτε οἰακίζει[xxv]
        - **Schleiermacher**: οἵη κυβερνήσει[xxvi]
        - **Schuster**: ἥτε οἵη τε κυβερνήσει[xxvii]
        - **Kahn**: ὅκη κυβερνῆσαι[xxviii]
    - Kirk, Raven, and Schofield note that ὁτέη ἐκυβέρνησε was likely to be ὅκη and render this as ὅκη κθβερνᾶται[xxix]

B 42 τόν τε Ὅμηρον ἔφασκεν ἄξιον ἐκ τῶν ἀγώνων ἐκβάλλεσθαι καὶ ῥαπίζεσθαι καὶ Ἀρχίλοχον ὁμοίως.

ἀγών, -ῶνος, ὁ: gathering, assembly
ἄξιος, -ία, -ιον: worthy, deserving to be
Ἀρχίλοχος: Archilochus, the lyric poet from Paros
ἐκ: (Prep. + Gen.) out of, from, forth from
ἐκβάλλω: to throw out, cast out, throw ashore, throw aside

Ὅμηρος, -ου, ὁ: Homer
ὁμοίως: (Adv.) similarly, likewise, unchangingly
ῥαπίζω: to strike with a stick, cudgel; slap in the face; beat, strike;
φάσκω: to think, say, affirm, assert

ἔφασκεν: 3rd Sg. Imp. Ind. Act. of φάσκω
ἀγώνων: Gen. Pl. Masc. of ἀγών
Ὅμηρον...ἄξιον... ἐκβάλλεσθαι καὶ ῥαπίζεσθαι: IS; *that Homer is worthy of being thrown out and struck with a stick/cudgel*

B 43 ὕβριν χρὴ σβεννύναι μᾶλλον ἢ πυρκαϊήν.

μάλα: (Adv.) much, very, exceedingly
πυρκαϊά, -ᾶς, ἡ: conflagration, arson, funeral pyre, burning pyre
σβέννυμι: to quench, put out, dry up, quell, check

ὕβρις, ὕβρεως, ἡ: insolence, wanton violence, outrage
χρὴ: (Impersonal + Inf.) it is necessary, one must, one ought, it must needs

σβεννύναι: Pres. Act. Inf. of σβέννθμι
μᾶλλον ἢ: (Comp. of μάλα+ ἢ) *more than*
πυρκαϊήν: Ionic Acc. Sg. of πυρκαϊά

B 44 μάχεσθαι χρὴ τὸν δῆμον ὑπὲρ τοῦ νόμου ὅκωσπερ τείχεος.

δῆμος, -ου, ὁ: land, district, country, people, inhabitants, government, township
μάχομαι: to quarrel, dispute, wrangle, contend, compete; (+ Dat.) to make war, fight, battle
νόμος, -ου, ὁ: practice, law, ordinance, custom, statute
ὅκωσπερ: Ionic, Conj. just as, in such a manner as, as

-περ: (Enclitic particle; added to end of a word) Untranslatable but adds force and emphasis
τεῖχος, τείχους, ὁ: city, mound, wall, fortification, fortress
ὑπὲρ: (Prep. + Gen.) over, on behalf of, in defense of, for the safety of, for the prosperity of
χρὴ: (Impersonal + Inf.) it is necessary, one must, one ought to, it must needs

μάχεσθαι: Pres. Mid./Pass. Inf. of μάχομαι
μάχεσθαι χρὴ τὸν δῆμον: IS; *it is necessary that the people fight*
τείχεος: Ionic Gen. Sg. of τεῖχος

B 45 ψυχῆς πείρατα ἰὼν οὐκ ἂν ἐξεύροιο πᾶσαν ἐπιπορευόμενος ὁδόν· οὕτω βαθὺν λόγον ἔχει.

ἂν: Used in conditionals; marks an indefinite; (w/ no Protasis) expresses what might have occurred in the past
βαθὺς, βαθεῖα, βαθύ: deep, profound, high, strong, copious, abundant
εἶμι: to go, go in, come, go through, enter
ἐξευρίσκω: to find out, discover
ἐπιπορεόμαι: travel
ἔχω: to have, hold

λόγος, -ου, ὁ: best to leave it as λόγος (or) as word, account, reason, understanding
ὁδός, ὁδοῦ, -ἡ: way, road, path, journey, trip, means, manner, method
οὐκ: (Particle) not, no
οὕτω(ς): (Adv.) so, thus, in this way, in this manner, so much, excessively
πᾶς, πᾶσα, πᾶν: all, every, each
πεῖραρ, -ατος, τό: end, limit
ψυχή, -ῆς, ἡ: soul, spirit, mind, ghost

ἰὼν: take appositively with the 2nd Sg. Subj. you; *you, going in,*
ἂν ἐξεύροιο: 2nd Sg. Aor. Mid. Opt.; *you would not discover*
πᾶσαν... ὁδόν: *whole way/entire way*
ἐπιπορευόμενος: Pres. Sg. Mid./Pass. Part.; *traveling*
οὕτω βαθὺν λόγον ἔχει: take ἔχει intransitively as meaning "to be;" *so deep is the λόγος*

B 46 τήν τε οἴησιν ἱερὰν νόσον ἔλεγε καὶ τὴν ὅρασιν ψεύδεσθαι

ἱερός, -ά, -όν: holy, divine, hallowed, supernatural
λέγω: say, speak, converse, tell a story
νόσος, -ου, ἡ: sickness, plague, disease, distress, anguish, bane, madness
οἴησις, -εως, ἡ: self-conceit

ὅρασις, -εως, ἡ: seeing, the act of sight, vision, power of sight
τε…καί: both…and
ψεύδω: to cheat, deceive, beguile, balk, disappoint; (Pass.) to be deceived, to be cheated

ἔλεγε: he (Heraclitus) said that
οἴησιν ἱερὰν νόσον: (Implied εἶναι in IS from ἔλεγε) self-conceit is a holy disease
ψεύδεσθαι: Pres. Mid./Pass. Inf. of ψεύδω; verb in IS with ὅρασιν as subject.

Notes:
- Burnet takes the ἱερὰν νόσον here as "falling sickness (epilepsy)" and Johnstone simply refers to it as "sacred disease (*epilepsy*)"

B 47 μὴ εἰκῆ περὶ τῶν μεγίστων συμβαλλώμεθα

εἰκῆ: at random, without plan, without purpose
μέγας, μεγάλη, μέγα: great, large, mighty, big, marvelous
μὴ: (Particle) no, not

περὶ: (+Gen.) concerning or about
συμβάλλω: conjecture, infer, conclude, interpret; *Literally*: to throw together

μεγίστων: Gen. Plural Superl. of μέγας, μεγάλη, μέγα
συμβαλλώμεθα: 1st Pl. Pres. Mid/Pass. Hort. Subj. of συμβάλλω; *let us not conjecture, infer*

B 48 τῷ οὖν τόξῳ ὄνομα βίος ἔργον δὲ θάνατος

βιός, -οῦ, ὁ: bow, bowmanship, archery
βίος, -ου, ὁ: life
ἔργον, -ου, τό: work, deed, industry, labor, action, proper work, business

θάνατος, -ου, ὁ: death
ὄνομα, ὀνόματος, τό: by name, name
οὖν: certainly, therefore, really, in fact
τόξον, -ου, τό: bow

> **ὄνομα βίος (ἐστίν)**: *the name for the bow is life*
> **δὲ**: take conjunctively as *but*
> **τῷ τόξῳ... ἔργον**: Take τῷ τόξῳ with the ἔργον as *work for the bow*

Notes:
- Heraclitus is making a pun between βίος (life) and βιός (bow)

B 49 εἷς ἐμοὶ μύριοι, <ἐὰν ἄριστος ᾖ>

ἄριστος, -η, -ον: best, noblest, greatest
ἐάν (+Subj.): if
ἐγώ: I

εἷς, μία, ἕν: (M. and N. Gen. Sg. ἑνός) one
μυρίος, -α, -ον: numberless, countless, infinite, measureless

> **εἷς...μύριοι**: *one man (would be worthy/equal to) countless men*
> **ἐμοί**: Dat. Sg. of ἐγώ; *to me*
> **ἐὰν...ᾖ**: Protasis of PGC; *if he were best*
> **ᾖ**: 3rd Sg. Pres. Subj. of εἰμί

B 49a ποταμοῖς τοῖς αὐτοῖς ἐμβαίνομέν τε καὶ οὐκ εἶμεν.

ποταμός, -οῦ, ὁ: river, stream
αὐτός, αὐτή, αὐτό: (With preceding definite article) same
ἐμβαίνω: to step in, go on, step upon, embark

τε: (Conj.) and, also, or untranslated
καί: (Conj.) and, even, also
οὐκ: (Particle) not, no

> **ποταμοῖς τοῖς αὐτοῖς**:(Art. + form of αὐτος = the same) *in the same rivers*
> **εἶμεν**: Epic 1st, Pl. Pres. of εἰμί
> **τε καὶ οὐκ εἶμεν**: *we both are and we are not*

B 50 Ἡ. μὲν οὖν <ἕν> φησιν εἶναι τὸ πᾶν διαιρετόν, γενητὸν ἀγένητον, θνητὸν ἀθάνατον, λόγον αἰῶνα, πατέρα υἱόν, θεὸν δίκαιον · οὐκ ἐμοῦ, ἀλλά τοῦ λόγου ἀκούσαντας ὁμολογεῖν σοφόν ἐστίν ἓν πάντα εἶναι.

ἀγένητος, -η, -ον: un-generated, uncreated
ἀθάνατος, -η, -ον: immortal, undying, everlasting, perpetual
αἰών, αἰῶνος, ὁ: time, epoch, eternity
ἀκούω: to hear something (Acc.); to hear from/of someone (+Gen.)
ἀλλά: (Conj.) but
γενητὸς, -ή, -όν: originated, generated
διαιρετός, -ή, -όν: separated, divided, distinguishable
δίκαιος, -ία, -ιον: just, righteous, lawful, right,
ἐγώ: I
ἐιμί: to be
εἷς, μία, ἕν: (Gen. ἑνός) one

θεός, οὗ, ὁ: god, deity
θνητός, -ή, -όν: mortal, human, mortal creature, one liable to death
λόγος, -ου, ὁ: best to leave it as λόγος (or) as word, account, reason, understanding
ὁμολογέω (ῶ): to agree with, correspond, agree to, concede, agree to do, promise to do
οὐ: (Particle) not, non
οὖν: certainly, therefore, really, in fact
πᾶς, πᾶσα, πᾶν: all, every, each
πατήρ, πατρός/πατέρος, ὁ: father
σοφός, -ή, -όν: wise, prudent, clever, shrewd, learned, universally and ideally wise, ingenious
υἱός, -οῦ, ὁ: son

Ἡ....φησιν εἶναι τὸ πᾶν διαιρετόν: IS; *Heraclitus says that everything is distinguishable*

γενητὸν ἀγένητον...θεὸν δίκαιον: Parallel structure as objects in IS; *(the generated is ungenerated...god is divine...*

ἐμοῦ: Gen. Sg. of ἐγώ

οὐκ ἐμοῦ, ἀλλά τοῦ λόγου ἀκούσαντας: *having not heard from me, but from the λόγος*[xxx]

σοφόν ἐστίν: Take impersonally; *it is wise (+Inf.)*

ὁμολογεῖν: *to agree that* (+Acc. and Inf. in IS, ἓν πάντα εἶναι)

B 51 οὐ ξυνιᾶσιν ὅκως διαφερόμενον ἑωυτῷ ὁμολογέει· παλίντροπος ἁρμονίη ὅκωσπερ τόξου καὶ λύρης.

ἁρμονία, -ας, ἡ: harmony, agreement, fastening, covenant

διαφέρω: to differ, carry different ways, quarrels, differs with

λύρα, -ας, ἡ: lyre

ὅκωσπερ: (Ionic, Conj.) just as, in such a manner as, as

ὁμολογεώ (ῶ): to agree with, correspond, agree to, concede, acknowledge, admit, agree to do, promise to do

ὅπως: (Adv.) as, in such manner as, how, just as, that, in the manner of; (Conj.) in order that

οὐ: (Particle) no, not

παλίντροπος, -η, -ον: contrary, turned away, averted

συνίημι: to understand, observe, notice (*lit:* "to send together")

τόξον, -ου, τό: bow

ξυνιᾶσιν: 3rd, Pres., Act., Pl. Ionic form of συνίημι; *they do not understand*
ὅκως: Ionic form of ὅπως; *that*
διαφερόμενον: *differing* (thing); subject of ὁμολογέει
ἑωυτῷ: Ionic Dat. Neuter/Masc. Sg. of ἑαυτοῦ; *with itself*
παλίντροπος, -η, -ον: *contrary (is) harmony* (ἁρμονίη)
ἁρμονίη: Ionic, Nom., Sg. of ἁρμονία
λύρης: Ionic, Sg. Fem. Gen. of λύρα

B 52 αἰὼν παῖς ἐστι παίζων, πεσσεύων · παιδός ἡ βασιληίη.

αἰών, αἰῶνος, ὁ: time, epoch, eternity
παῖς, παιδός, ὁ/ἡ: child, kid, son, daughter, boy, girl
παίζω: to play (a game), to play a sport

πεσσεύω: to play at draughts
βασιλεία, -ᾱς, ἡ: kingdom, dominion

παιδός: Possessive Gen. of παῖς
βασιληίη: Ion. Nom. Sg. form of βασιλεία; *the kingdom/dominion (is) a child's*

B 53 πόλεμος πάντων μέν πατήρ ἐστι, πάντων δὲ βασιλεύς, καὶ τοὺς μὲν θεοὺς ἔδειξε τοὺς δὲ ἀνθρώπους, τοὺς μὲν δούλους ἐποίησε τούς δὲ ἐλευθέρους.

ἄνθρωπος, -ου, ὁ: man, human
βασιλεύς, βασιλέως, ὁ: king, master, chief, lord, patron
δέ: (Particle) but on the other hand, but, or just leave untranslated
δείκνυμι: to show, make known, point out, prove, displayed
δοῦλος, -ου, ὁ: slave, bondman, serf
ἐλευθέρος, -α, -ον: free, independent

θεός, -οῦ, ὁ: god, divine, deity
μέν: (Particle) on the one hand, while, whereas, or just leave untranslated
πᾶς, πᾶσα, πᾶν: all, every, each
πατήρ, πατρός/πατέρος, ὁ: father
ποιέω (-ῶ): make, do, act, produce, cause
πόλεμος, -ου, ὁ: war, conflict, battle

ἔδειξε: 3rd Sg. Aor. Act. Indic.; πόλεμος is the assumed subject; *it showed*
τοὺς μὲν...τοὺς δὲ: *some as...others as*
ἐποίησε: 3rd Sg. Aor. Act. Indic.; πόλεμος is the assumed subject; *it made*

B 54 ἁρμονίη ἀφανὴς φανερῆς κρείττων.

ἀγαθός, -ή, -όν: good
ἁρμονία, -ας, ἡ: harmony, concord, agreement
ἀφανής, -ές: unseen, unnoticed, out of sight, invisible

κρατύς, -εῖα,-υ: strong, mighty
φανερός: visible, manifest, evident, apparent

ἁρμονίη: Ionic form of ἁρμονία; *unseen harmony*
φανερῆς: Ionic Fem. Gen. Sg. of φανερός; Gen. of Comp. from κρείττων; *than the visible*
κρείττων: Nom. Sg. Comp. of either κρατύς or ἀγαθός;

B 55 ὅσων ὄψις ἀκοὴ μάθησις, ταῦτα ἐγὼ προτιμέω.

ἀκοή , -ῆς, -ἡ: hearing, listening; something heard, hearsay
ἐγώ: I
μάθησις, -εως, ἡ: learning, education
οὗτος, αὕτη, τοῦτο: this; (pl.) those, these

ὅσος, -η, -ον: (Adj.) how many, as much as, so far as, so many as
ὄψις, -εως, ἡ: sight, appearance, aspect
προτιμάω (-ῶ): to honor, prefer, wish, take heed of

ὅσων: Gen. Pl. N. of ὅσος; *of however many things (there are for)...*ὄψις...μάθησις
ταῦτα: N. Pl. of οὗτος, αὕτη, τοῦτο; *these things...*ἐγὼ προτιμέω
προτιμέω: Ionic 1st Sg. Pres. Act. Ind. of προτιμάω

B 56

1 ἐξηπάτηνται οἱ ἄνθρωποι πρὸς τὴν γνῶσιν τῶν φανερῶν παραπλησίως Ὁμήρωι, ὃς
2 ἐγένετο τῶν Ἑλλήνων σοφώτερος πάντων. ἐκεῖνόν τε γὰρ παῖδες φθεῖρας
3 κατακτείνοντες ἐξηπάτησαν εἰπόντες· ὅσα εἴδομεν καὶ ἐλάβομεν, ταῦτα ἀπολείπομεν,
4 ὅσα δὲ οὔτε εἴδομεν οὔτ᾽ ἐλάβομεν, ταῦτα φέρομεν.

ἄνθρωπος, -ου, ὁ: man, human
ἀπολείπω: to leave behind, desert
γάρ: (Conjunction) for, since
γνῶσις, -εως, ἡ: knowledge,
δέ: (Particle) but on the other hand, but, or just leave untranslated
γίγνομαι: to become; to be born; to come to be
εἶδον: to see
εἶπον: (Aor. 1st. Sg. Ind.) to say, speak
ἐκεῖνος, ἐκείνη, ἐκεῖνο: (Demon. Pro.) that person/thing there; that person/thing; (Pl.) those people/things
λαμβάνω: to take, grasp, seize
Ἑλλήν: Hellenes
ἐξαπατάω: to deceive
καί: (Conj.) and, even, also

κατακτείνω: to kill, slay
Ὅμηρος, -ου, ὁ: Homer
ὅς, ἥ, ὅ: (Relative Pronoun) who, which
ὅσος, -α, -ον: whatever, what
οὔτε...οὔτε: (Correl.) neither...nor
παῖς, παιδός, ὁ/ἡ: child, kid, son, daughter, boy, girl
πᾶς, πᾶσα, πᾶν: all, every, each
παραπλησίος, -α, -ον: in the same manner, just as, equally
πρός: (+Acc.) over, by
σοφός, -ή, -όν: wise, prudent, clever, shrewd, learned, universally and ideally wise, ingenious
οὗτος, αὕτη, τοῦτο: this; (pl.) those, these
φανερός: visible, manifest, evident, apparent
φέρω: to bring, bear, carry
φθείρ, φθειρός, ὁ: louse; (pl.) lice

1 ἐξηπάτηνται: 3rd Pl. Perf. Mid./Pas.; Subj. is οἱ ἄνθρωποι
παραπλησίως Ὁμήρωι: in a similar matter to Homer
ὅς: Masc. Sg. Nom. Rel. Pronoun
2 τῶν Ἑλλήνων. σοφώτερος πάντων: Comp. + Gen. of Comparison; wiser than all the Greeks
3 κατακτείνοντες: Pres. Act. Pl. Part. of κατακτείνω
φθεῖρας κατακτείνοντες: killing lice
ἐξηπάτησαν: 3rd Pl. Aor. Ind. Act.; deceived (+ἐκεῖνόν as acc. obj.)
ἐκεῖνόν: Antecedent is Ὁμήρωι or Homer
εἴδομεν...ἐλάβομεν: 1st Pl. Aor. Act. Forms
4 ἀπολείπομεν...φέρομεν: 1st. Pl. Pres. Forms

B 57 διδάσκαλος δὲ πλείστων Ἡσίοδος; τοῦτον ἐπίστανται πλεῖστα εἰδέναι, ὅστις ἡμέρην καί εὐφρόνην οὐκ ἐγίνωσκεν; ἔστι γάρ ἕν.

γιγνώσκω: to know, perceive, understand, be aware of

δέ: (Particle) but on the other hand, but, or just leave untranslated

διδάσκαλος, -ου, ὁ: teacher, master

εἷς, μία, ἕν: one

ἐπίσταμαι: to know, be able, to be assured, observe, understand

εὐφρόνη, -ης, ἡ: night (Lit: the kindly/good time)

ἡμέρα, -ας, ἡ: day; a particular day; each day

Ἡσίοδος, -ου, ὁ: Hesiod (~700 BC); one of the two most famous ancient Greek Epic poets; his works included the *Theogony* and *Works and Days*

οἶδα: (Perf. translated as Pres.) I know

ὅστις, ἥτις, ὅτι: whoever, anyone, anything which, whichsoever, whatsoever, anything, he/she who, it which

οὐκ: (Particle) not, no

πλεῖστος, -η, -ον: Superl. of πολύς, πολλή, πολύ; most, greatest, largest, greatest number

πλείστων: (Partitive Gen.) *of most people*

τοῦτον ἐπίστανται πλεῖστα εἰδέναι: Ind. Statement; *they are assured that this man (τοῦτον) knew most things*

εἰδέναι: Perf. Act. Inf. of οἶδα

ὅστις: referring to Hesiod

ἐγίνωσκεν: Ionic 3rd Sg. Imp. form of γιγνώσκω

B 58 καὶ ἀγαθὸν καὶ κακόν. οἱ γοῦν ἰατροί, τέμνοντες, καίοντες, πάντη βασανίζοντες κακῶς τοὺς ἀρρωστοῦντας, ἐπαιτέονται μηδὲν ἄξιοι μισθὸν λαμβάνειν παρὰ τῶν ἀρρωστούντων, ταὐτὰ ἐργαζόμενοι, τὰ ἀγαθὰ καὶ τὰς νόσους.

ἀγαθός, -ή, -όν: good, noble, brave, fortunate
ἄξιος, -ία, -ιον: worthy, deserving to be
ἀρρωστέω (ῶ): to be unwell, ill
βασανίζω: to torture, examine
γοῦν: (Compound Particle of γε οὖν) at least then, at all events
ἐπαιτέω (ῶ): to ask besides, beg, demand
ἐργάζομαι: to work at, labor, make
ἰατρός, -οῦ, ὁ: doctor, physician
καί: (Conj.) and, even, also
καίω: to kindle, ignite, set on fire

κακός, -ή, όν: wicked, evil, mean, ugly, ignoble, base, baneful, bad
λαμβάνω: to seize, take hold of; catch, overtake
μηδείς, μηδεμία, μηδέν: no one, nothing
μισθός, οῦ, ὁ: wages, pay
νόσος, -ου, ἡ: sickness, plague, disease, distress, anguish, bane, madness
οὗτος, αὕτη, τοῦτο: this; (pl.) those, these
παρά: (Prep. + Gen) from, beside
πᾶς, πασα, πᾶν: all, every, each, whole
τέμνω: to cut, wound, maim

τέμνοντες...ἐργαζόμενοι: All Part. here are Pres. Act.
πάντη: Dat. Sg.; *in every way*
ἐπαιτέονται: 3rd Pl. Pres. Mid./Pas. Ind. of ἐπαιτέω
ἐπαιτέονται...μισθὸν λαμβάνειν: IS; *demand that they receive a wage*
μηδὲν ἄξιοι: ἄξιοι has ἰατροί as its antecedent; *worthy of nothing*
παρὰ τῶν ἀρρωστούντων: Prep. + Gen. Attributive Part.; *from the sick people*
ταὐτά: Crasis of τὰ αὐτὰ; *the same things*

B 59 γναφείῳ ὁδὸς εὐθεῖα καὶ σκολιὴ μία ἐστί, (φησί,) καὶ ἡ αὐτή.

αὐτός, -ή, -όν: (Art. + αὐτός, -ή, -όν) the same
γναφεῖον, -ου, τό: fuller (someone who spins and cleans wool or cloth)
εἷς, μία, ἕν: one

εὐθύς, -εῖα, -ύ: straight, direct
καί: (Conj.) and, even, also
ὁδός, -οῦ, ἡ: way, road, path
σκολιός, -ά, -όν: bent, curved, crooked

γναφείῳ: Dat. of Reference[xxxi]; Sg. of γναφεῖον; *for writing*
σκολιὴ: Ionic F. Sg. Nom. of σκολιά

B 60 ὁδός ἄνω κάτω μία καὶ ὡυτή.

ἄνω: (Adv.) (With Verbs implying Motion) upwards, up, on the upper side
εἷς, μία, ἕν: one

κάτω: (Adv.) (With Verbs implying Motion) downwards, down, below, southward, lower
ὁδός, ὁδοῦ, -ἡ: way, road, path, journey, trip, means, manner, method

ἄνω (καὶ) κάτω (ἐστὶν) μία: *up and down is one*
καὶ: *and*
ὡυτή: Fem. Adj. Nom. Sg. for ὁ αὐτός; *the same*

B 61 ---- ---- θάλασσα ὕδωρ καθαρώτατον καὶ μιαρώτατον, ἰχθύσι μὲν πότιμον καὶ σωτήριον, ανθρώποις δὲ ἄποτον καὶ ὀλέθριον.

ἄνθρωπος,-ου, ὁ: man, human, person
ἄποτος, -ον: not drinkable, not drunk from, never delivering, not drinking, unable to drink
θάλασσα, -ης, ἡ: sea, sea-water, salt-water
ἰχθύς, ἰχθύος, ὁ: fish
καθαρός, -ά, -όν: clean, pure (especially of water)
μέν...δέ: on the one hand...on the other hand

μιαρός, -ά, -όν: polluted, abominable, foul, defiled, repulsive, unclean
πότιμος, -α, -ον: drinkable, fresh
ὀλέθριος, -ον: destructive, deadly, fatal, bringing ruin
σωτήριος, -ον: saving, delivering, bringing safety
ὕδωρ, ὕδατος, τό: water

καθαρώτατον: N. Sg. Superl. of καθαρόν; *purest* or *cleanest*
μιαρώτατον: N. Sg. Superl. of μιαρόν; *most polluted* or *foulest*
ἰχθύσι μὲν... ανθρώποις δὲ: both are Datives of Reference; *for fish...for men*
πότιμον... ἄποτον καὶ ὀλέθριον: N. Sg. Nom/Acc. from the ὕδωρ

50

B 62 ἀθάνατοι θνητοί, θνητοὶ ἀθάνατοι ζῶντες τὸν ἐκείνων θάνατον, τὸν δὲ ἐκείνων βίον τεθνεῶτες.

ἀθάνατος, -η, -ον: immortal, undying, everlasting, perpetual
βίος, -ου, ὁ: life
δέ: (Particle) but, but on the other hand, or just leave untranslated
ἐκεῖνος, ἐκείνη, ἐκεῖνο: (Demon. Pro.) that person/thing there; that person/thing; (Pl.) those people/things

ζάω (-ῶ): to live
θάνατος, -ου, ὁ: death
θνήσκω: to die, to be dying
θνητός, -ή, -όν: mortal, human, mortal creature, one liable to death

ἀθάνατοι (εἰσι) θνητοί, θνητοὶ (εἰσι)ἀθάνατοι: [+Implied εἰσι(ν)] *immortals are mortals (and) mortals are immortals*
ζῶντες: Pres. Pl. Masc. Act. Part.; *living*
τεθνεῶτες: Perf. Pl. Masc. Act. Part.; *having died* or *having finished*

B 63 λέγει δὲ καὶ σαρκὸς ἀνάστασιν ταύτης <τῆς> φανερᾶς, ἐνῇ γεγενήμεθα, καὶ τὸν θεὸν οἶδε ταύτης τῆς ἀναστάσεως αἴτιον οὕτως λέγων· ἔνθα δ' ἐόντι ἐπανίστασθαι καὶ φύλακας γίνεσθαι ἐγερτὶ ζώντων καὶ νεκρῶν.

αὐτός, -ή, -όν: (Art + form of αὐτός, -ή, -ον) the same
γίγνομαι: become, come into being, be born, be produced
δέ: (Particle) but, but on the other hand, or just leave untranslated
διά: (Prep. + Gen.) through, throughout, along
ἐγερτί: (Adv.) busily, eagerly
ἐν: (Prep. + Dat.) in, on, at, among
ἔνθα: (Adv.) there, thither
ἐπανίστημι: to set up again, make rise against
ζάω (-ῶ): to live

καί: (Conj.) and, even, also
κόσμος, -ου, ὁ: order, world, universe, earth
κρίσις, -εως, ἡ: decision, judgment, choice
λέγω: say, speak, converse, tell a story
νεκρός, -οῦ, ὁ: corpse, dead body
οὕτως: (Adv.) so, thus, in this way
πᾶς, πασα, πᾶν: all, every, each, whole
πῦρ, πυρός, τό: fire; funeral-fire, sacrificial fire, hearthfire
φύλαξ, -ακος, ὁ: guard, watcher, sentry

ἐόντι: Dat. Sg. Pres. Act. Part. of εἰμί; *in essence*
ἐπανίστασθαι: Pres. Mid./Pass. Inf. of ἐπανίστημι
ἐπανίστασθαι καὶ φύλακας: *(Heraclitus says that) guards arise*
γίνεσθαι: Ionic, Pres. Mid./Pass. Inf. of γίγνομαι
ζώντων: Attributive[xxxii] Gen. Pl. Pres. Act. Part.; *of the living*

51

B 64 τὰ δὲ πάντα οἰακίζει κεραυνός.

αὐτός, -ή, -όν: (Article + form of αὐτός, -ή, -όν)
the same
δέ: (Particle) but, but on the other hand, or just
leave untranslated
κατευθύνω: to steer, direct, guide

κεραυνός, -οῦ, ὁ: thunderbolt
οἰακίζω: to steer, govern, manage, guided
πᾶς, πᾶσα, πᾶν: all, every, each, whole

οἰακίζει: 3rd Sg. Pres. Ind. Act. of οἰακίζω

B 65 καλεῖ δὲ αὐτὸ χρησμοσύνην καὶ κόρον

δέ: (Particle) but, but on the other hand, or just
leave untranslated
καί: (Conj.) and, even, also
καλέω: to call, summon

κόρος, -ου, ὁ: excess, surfeit, satiety
χρησμοσύνη, -ης, ἡ: poverty, need, want

(Ἡ. καλεῖ)...: IS; *(Heraclitus calls it (αὐτὸ)* + Acc.

> **Notes:**
> - Robinson claims that αὐτό here refers to fire, as does Burnet
> - Wheeelright (fragment 30 in his edition) contends that the αὐτὸ refers to the "phases of fire," which are χρησμοσύνην καὶ κόρον[xxxiii]

B 66 πάντα γάρ, φησί, τὸ πῦρ ἐπελθὸν κρινεῖ καὶ καταλήψεται.

γάρ: (Conj.) for, since
ἐπέρχομαι: to come upon, come neat, come
against, come on, return,
καταλαμβάνω: to seize, lay hold of
κρίνω: to separate, put asunder, distinguish, pick
out, choose, judge, decide

πᾶς, πᾶσα, πᾶν: all, every, each, whole
πῦρ, πυρός, τό: fire; funeral-fire, sacrificial fire,
hearthfire
φημί: to say, speak, agree

φησί: 3rd Pl. Pres. Act. Ind. of φημί
ἐπελθὸν: Aor. Nom. Sg. Neut. Act. Part. of ἐπέρχομαι ; *having come upon/ having come against*
κρινεῖ: 3rd Sg. Fut. Act. Ind. Contract of κρίνω
καταλήψεται: 3rd Sg. Fut. Act. Ind. of καταλαμβάνω

B 67 ὁ θεὸς ἡμέρη εὐφρόνη, χειμὼν θέρος, πόλεμος εἰρήνη, κόρος λιμός (τἀναντία ἅπαντα· οὗτος ὁ νοῦς), ἀλλοιοῦται δὲ ὅκωσπερ (πῦρ), ὁπόταν συμμιγῇ θυώμασιν ὀνομάζεται καθ᾽ ἡδονὴν ἑκάστου.

ἀλλοιόω: to change, alter
ἅπας, ἅπασα, ἅπαν: all, the whole, everything, all together
δέ: (Particle) but, but on the other hand, or just leave untranslated
εἰρήνη, -ης, ἡ: peace
ἕκαστος, -η, -ον: each, every
ἐναντίος, -α, -ον: opposite, contrary, reverse
εὐφρόνη, -ης, ἡ: night time
ἡδονή, -ῆς, ἡ: pleasure, delight
ἡμέρα, -ας, ἡ: day
θεὸς, -οῦ, ὁ: deity, god, divine
θέρος, -εος, τό: summer
θύωμα, -ατος, τό: something burnt as incense; (Pl.) spices

κατά: (+Acc.) according to, corresponding with, after the fashion of
κόρος, -ου, ὁ: satisfaction, satiety, excess, abundance
λιμός, -οῦ, ὁ: hunger, famine
νοῦς, νοῦ, ὁ: mind intelligence, wit
ὅκωσπερ: Ionic, Conj. just as, in such a manner as, as
ὀνομάζω: to call, name, specify
ὁπόταν: (Adv.) whenever, whensoever (+ Subj.)
οὗτος, αὕτη, τοῦτο: this; (pl.) those, these
πόλεμος, -ου, ὁ: war, conflict, battle
πῦρ, πυρός, τό: fire; funeral-fire, sacrificial fire, hearth fire
συμμίγνυμι: to mix together, commingle
χειμών, -ῶνος, ὁ: winter, cold, frost

ἡμέρη (ἐστίν) εὐφρόνη: Implied ἐστι(ν) in between each of the noun pairs (ἡμέρη... λιμός)
συμμιγῇ: 3rd Sg. Pres. Mid./Pass. Subj. of συμμίγνυμι; Subj. from ὁπόταν; *mingled with spices* (Dat. Pl. θυώμασιν)
ἀλλοιοῦται: 3rd Sg. Pres. Ind. of ἀλλοιόω
τἀναντία: Crasis of τὰ ἐναντία; N. Pl. Acc.; *the opposites*

B 68 καὶ διὰ τοῦτο εἰκότως αὐτὰ ἄκεα Ἡ. προσεῖπεν ὡς ἐξακεσόμενα τὰ δεινὰ καὶ τὰς ψυχὰς ἐξάντεις ἀπεργαζόμενα τῶν ἐν τῆι γενέσει συμφορῶν.

ἄκος, -εος, τό: cure, remedy
ἀντάω: to go opposite, come opposite to, meet face to facee
ἀπεργάζομαι: to finish off, complete
αὐτός, -ή, -όν: (Art. + form of αὐτός, -ή, -όν) the same
γένεσις, -εως, ἡ: birth, origin, beginning, genesis
δεινός, ή, όν: powerful, fearful, terrible
διά: (Prep. + Acc.) through, on account of, because of, thanks to, by the aid of

εἰκότως: (Adv.) suitably, reasonably
ἐν: (Prep. + Dat.) in, on, at, among
ἐξακέομαι: to heal completely, appease
καί: (Conj.) and, even, also
προσεῖπον: to address, speak to, call, name
συμφορά, -ῆς, ἡ: misfortune, punishment, disease
οὗτος, αὕτη, τοῦτο: this; (Pl.) those, these
ψυχή, -ῆς, ἡ: soul, spirit, mind, life, ghost
ὡς: (as an Adv.) as, just as, so, thus, when

εἰκότως αὐτὰ ἄκεα Ἡ. προσεῖπεν: *Heraclitus reasonably called these (things) remedies*
ἐξακεσόμενα: Part. Pl. Fut. Mid. Part. of ἐξακέομαι
ὡς ἐξακεσόμενα τὰ δεινὰ καὶ τὰς ψυχὰς: *as the powerful (remedies) will heal even the souls*
ἐξάντεις: 2ⁿᵈ Sg. Pres. Act. Ind. of ἀντάω
ἀπεργαζόμενα: Pres. N. Pl. Part. of ἀπεργάζομαι
ἐν τῆι γενέσει συμφορῶν: *in the beginning of misfortunes*

Notes:

- Robinson does not include this fragment in his edition of the fragments, noting that this fragment, like 69, 70, and 71 following it appear to be the author's "vague summary or reminiscence of some Heraclitean saying."[xxxiv]
- Kahn lists this fragment in his Appendix I, noting that that this fragment seems rather devoid of relevant context.[xxxv]
- The Red text above are not translated by Kahn[xxxvi] and Freeman[xxxvii] but are still included in the Dielz-Kranz text itself. These translators and commentators focus on the ἄκεα.

B 69 θυσιῶν τοίνυν τίθημι διττὰ εἴδη· τὰ μὲν τῶν ἀποκεκαθαρμένων παντάπασιν ἀνθρώπων, οἷα ἐφ' ἑνὸς ἄν ποτε γένοιτο σπανίως, ὥς φησιν Ἡ., ἢ τινων ὀλίγων εὐαριθμήτων ἀνδρῶν·

ἄν: (Particle) used to indicate limitation or mode
ἀνήρ, ἀνδρός, ὁ: man, human being
ἄνθρωπος, -ου, ὁ: man, human
ἀποκαθαίρω: to clear, cleanse
διττός, -ή, -όν: twofold, double
εἶδος, -εος, τό: form, kind; (Literally: that which is seen)
εἷς, μία, ἕν: (Gen. ἑνός) one
ἐπί: (Prep. + Gen.) in, in the presence of
εὐαρίθμητος, -ον: easy to count, few in number
ἤ: (Conj.) or

θυσία, -ας, ἡ: sacrifice, offering, victim
μέν: (Particle) on the one hand, while, whereas, or just leave untranslated
οἷος, οἵα, οἷον: just as, as; such as
ὀλίγος, -η, -ον: few, little, low
παντάπασιν: (Adv.) all in al, altogether, wholly
πότε: (Enclitic Particle) at some time, at another time
σπανίος, -α, -ον: rare, scant, scarce
τίθημι: to set, set up, assign, reckon
τις, τις, τι, (Gen.: τινος): anyone, anything, someone, something
τοίνυν: therefore, accordingly, then

εἴδη: N. Pl. of εἶδος
ἀποκεκαθαρμένων: Gen. Pl. Perf. Mid./Pass. Part. of ἀποκαθαίρω
τὰ μὲν τῶν ἀποκεκαθαρμένων... ἀνθρώπων: *some of those men having been cleansed*
ἐφ' ἑνός: *in the case of an individual (or a single person)*
γένοιτο: 3rd Sg. Aor. Opt. Mid. of γίγνομαι; N. Pl. of οἷα (whose antecedent is the preceding τὰ) is the Subject
σπανίως: (Adv.) rarely, scarcely

B 70 πόσωι δὴ οὖν βέλτιον Ἡ. παίδων ἀθύρματα νενόμικεν εἶναι τὰ ἀνθρώπινα δοξάσματα.

ἄθυρμα, ἀθύρματος, τό: toy, plaything, adornment, delighy
ἀνθρώπινος, -η, -ον: relating to humans, humanlike
δόξασμα, δοξάσματος, τό: opinion, notion,

νομίζω: to believe, think, esteem, acknowledge
παῖς, παιδός, ὁ/ἡ: child, kid, son, daughter, boy, girl

πόσωι δὴ οὖν βέλτιον Ἡ(ράκλειτος): Heraclitus as subject: *greater by a certain magnitude, Heraclitus*
παίδων: Part. Gen. with ἀθύρματα; *playthings of kids/children*
νενόμικεν: 3rd Sg. Plup. Act. Ind. of νομίζω; H. (Heraclitus) is the subject here
νενόμικεν...εἶναι: IS; *he had thought that...are*

B 71 μεμνῆσθαι δὲ καὶ τοῦ ἐπιλανθανομένου ᾗ ἡ ὁδὸς ἄγει.

ἄγω: to lead, guide
δέ: (Particle) but, but on the other hand, or just leave untranslated
ἐπιλανθάνομαι: to forget

καί: (Conj.) and, even, also
μιμνήσκω: to remind, put in mind; (+ Gen.) remember, mention
ὁδός, -οῦ, ἡ: way, road, path

μεμνῆσθαι: Perf. Mid./Pas. Inf. of μιμνήσκω
μεμνῆσθαι... ἐπιλανθανομένου: *to have been reminded of the man forgetting*
ἐπιλανθανομένου: Pres. Gen. Sg. Mid./Pas. Part. of ἐπιλανθάνομαι
ᾗ: Dat. Fem. Sg. Rel. Pro.; *where, on which way, in which*

B 72 ᾧι μάλιστα διηνεκῶς ὁμιλοῦσι λόγωι τῶι τὰ ὅλα διοικοῦντι τούτωι διαφέρονται, καὶ οἷς καθ᾽ ἡμέραν ἐγκυροῦσι, ταῦτα αὐτοῖς ξένα φαίνεται.

διαφέρω: to quarrel with, be at variance with (+ Dat.)
διηνεκής, -ές: unbroken, continuous
διοικέω: to manage, govern, administer, furnish, control
ἐγκύρω: to meet with (+ Gen.)
ἡμέρα, -ας, ἡ: day; particular day; each day
καί: (Conj.) and, even, also
μάλιστα: (Superl.) best, most, above all
ξένος, -η, -ον: foreign, strange, unusual

ὄγος, -ου, ὁ: best to leave it as λόγος (or) as word, account, reason, understanding
ὅς, ἥ, ὅ: (Relative Pronoun) who, which
ὅλος, -α, -ον: all, the whole; (as N. Substantive) the universe, all things, everything
ὁμιλέω: to be in contact with, be acquainted with, associate with
φαίνω: (+ Pred. Adj.) appear, come into being, bring to light, shows, displays

τούτωι διαφέρονται: *they are at variance with this thing which* (ᾧι...τούτωι)
ᾧι μάλιστα διηνεκῶς ὁμιλοῦσι λόγωι: *they are in contact with the λόγος most continuously*
ᾧι: Dat. Sg M./N. Rel. Pro.
διοικοῦντι: Pres. Act. Dat. Part. of διοικέω
τῶι τὰ ὅλα διοικοῦντι: Attrib. Part. Phrase with Dat. Sg. Antecedent λόγωι; *the one furnishing all things*
καθ᾽ ἡμέραν: Idiom for *every day* (Literally: *for the day*)
ταῦτα αὐτοῖς ξένα φαίνεται: Dat. of Reference[xxxviii]; *these things appear foreign to them*

B 73 οὐ δεῖ ὥσπερ καθεύδοντας ποιεῖν καὶ λέγειν· καὶ γὰρ καὶ τότε δοκοῦμεν ποιεῖν καὶ λέγειν.

γάρ: (Conj.) for, since
δεῖ: (w/Acc. or Infin.) it is necessary, it is needful for one to do, one must
δοκέω (-ῶ): to seem; to think, suppose, imagine
καθεύδω: sleep, lie down to sleep, lie idle, sleep away, pass the night, lie

καί: (Conj.) and, even, also
λέγω: say, speak, converse, tell a story
οὐ: (Particle) no, not
ποιέω (-ῶ): make, do, act, produce, cause
τότε: (Adv.) then, at that time
ὥσπερ: (Adv. of Manner) just as, even as, like as

> **οὐ δεῖ... ποιεῖν καὶ λέγειν**: *one ought not act and speak*
> **καθεύδοντας**: Pres. Acc. Pl. Act. Participle
> **ὥσπερ καθεύδοντας**: *just as those sleeping*
> **δοκοῦμεν**: 1st Pl. Pres. Act. Ind. Cont. form of δοκέω

B 74 οὐ δεῖ (ὡς) παῖδας τοκεών.

δεῖ: (w/Acc. or Infin.) it is necessary, it is needful for one to do, one must
οὐ: (Particle) not, no
παῖς, παιδός, ὁ/ἡ: child, kid, son, daughter, boy, girl

παραλαμβάνω: to receive from;
τοκεύς, -έως, ὁ: parent
ὡς: (as an Adv.) as, just as, so, thus, when,

> **οὐ δεῖ... παῖδας**: Acc. Pl. can be subject of impersonal δεῖ; *children ought not*
> **τοκεών**: Gen. Pl. of τοκεύς; Gen. Obj. of δεῖ; *(be like) their parents*

B 75 τοὺς καθεύδοντας οἶμαι ὁ ῾Η. ἐργάτας εἶναι λέγει καὶ συνεργοὺς τῶν ἐν τῷ κόσμῳ γινομένων.

γίγνομαι: become, come into being, be born, be produced
ἐν: (Prep. + Dat.) in, on, at, among
ἐργάτης, -ου, ὁ: worker, laborer,
καθεύδω: sleep, lie down to sleep, lie idle, sleep away, pass the night, lie

κόσμος, -ου, ὁ: order, world, universe, earth
λέγω: say, speak, converse, tell a story
οἴομαι: to think, conjecture, suppose, expect
συνεργός, -ά, -όν: working together, joining; (+Gen.) taking part in

καθεύδοντας: Pl. Pres. Acc. Part. of καθεύδω
οἶμαι ὁ ῾Η.... εἶναι λέγει: IS; *I think Heraclitus...says that* (+ τοὺς καθεύδοντας)
τοὺς καθεύδοντας: Attrib. Part.; *the ones asleep* or *those asleep are* ἐργάτας... καὶ συνεργοὺς
ἐργάτας... συνεργοὺς: *laborers...and those taking part in* (+ τῶν...γινομένων)
γινομένω: Pl. Pres. Gen. Part. of γίγνομαι

B 76 ζῇ πῦρ τὸν ἀέρος θάνατον καὶ ἀὴρ ζῇ τὸν πυρὸς θάνατον, ὕδωρ ζῇ τὸν γῆς θάνατον, γῆ τὸν ὕδατος.

ἀήρ, ἀέρος, ὁ: air
γῆ, γῆς, ἡ: earth, soil, land
ζάω (-ῶ): to live

θάνατος, -ου, ὁ: death
πῦρ, πυρός, τό: fire; funeral-fire, sacrificial fire, hearth fire
ὕδωρ, ὕδατος, τό: water

ζῇ: 3rd Sg. Ind. Act. of ζάω (-ῶ); *fire lives the death*

58

B 77 ὅθεν καὶ Ἡράκλειτον ψυχῇσι φάναι τέρψιν ἢ θάνατον ὑγρῇσι γενέσθαι, τέρψιν δὲ εἶναι αὐταῖς τὴν εἰς γένεσιν πτῶσιν, ἀλλαχοῦ δὲ φάναι ζῆν ἡμᾶς τὸν ἐκείνων θάνατον καὶ ζῆν ἐκείνας τὸν ἡμέτερον θάνατον.

ἀλλαχοῦ: (Adv.) elsewhere

αὐτός, -ή, -όν: (Art. + form of αὐτός, -ή, -όν) the same

γένεσις, -εως, ἡ: origin genesis

γίγνομαι: become, come into being, be born, be produced

δέ: (Particle) but, but on the other hand, or just leave untranslated

εἰς: (Prep + Acc.) into, onto, up to, until

ἐκεῖνος, ἐκείνη, ἐκεῖνο: (Demon. Pro.) that (Pl.) those

ζάω (-ῶ): to live

ἤ: (Conj.) or

ἡμεῖς: (Pronoun) we

ἡμέτερος, -α, -ον: our, ours

θάνατος, -ου, ὁ: death

καί: (Conj.) and, even, also

ὅθεν: (Adv.) whence

πτῶσις, -εως, ἡ: falling, fall, arrangement

τέρψις, -εως, ἡ: enjoyment, pleasure, delight

ὑγρός, - ά, -όν: wet, moist, fluid

φημί: to say, speak, agree

ψυχή, -ῆς, ἡ: soul, spirit, mind, life, ghost

ὅθεν καὶ Ἡράκλειτον... φάναι: *whence (it is said that) Heraclitus says that*
φάναι: Pres. Act. Inf. of φημί
ψυχῇσι: Dat. Pl. *for souls*
ὑγρῇσι γενέσθαι: *to become wet*

B 78 ἦθος γὰρ ἀνθρώπειον μὲν οὐκ ἔχει γνώμας, θεῖον δὲ ἔχει.

ἀνθρώπειος, -α, -ον: human, suited to man, within man's powers

γάρ: (Conjunction) for, since

γνώμη, -ης, ὁ: understanding, means of knowing, intelligence, thought, judgement;

ἔχω: to have, hold

ἦθος, -εος, τό: disposition, character, custom, usage

θεῖος, -α, -ον: of or from the gods, divine, sacred, holy

μέν...δέ: on the one hand...on the other hand

οὐκ: (Particle) not, no

γνώμας: LSJ takes γνώμας as "practical maxims" or *understanding*
θεῖον δὲ ἔχει: *but divine (ἦθος) does have it (γνώμας)*

B 79 ἀνὴρ νήπιος ἤκουσε πρὸς δαίμονος ὅκωσπερ παῖς πρὸς ἀνδρός.

ἀκούω: to hear something (Acc.); to hear from/of someone (+Gen.)

ἀνήρ, ἀνδρός, ὁ: man, male

δαίμων,-ονος, ὁ/ἡ: god, goddess, divine power, deity, fortune, spirit

νήπιος, -η, -ον: childish, infantile, silly, blind, without foresight

ὅπως: (Adv.) as, in such manner as, how, just as; (Conj.) in order that

-περ: (Enclitic particle; added to end of a word) Untranslatable but adds force and emphasis παῖς, παιδός, ὁ/ἡ: child, kid, son, daughter, boy, girl

πρὸς: (+Gen) before, in the presence of from, at, to; on the side of, in the direction of

ἤκουσε: 3ʳᵈ Sg. Aor. Act. Indic.; intransitive, pass. as either *hear oneself called*, *is called*

πρός: *before, in the presence of*, or *in comparison to*

ὅκως: Ionic form of ὅπως

ὅκωσπερ: *just as*

B 80 εἰδέναι δὲ χρὴ τὸν πόλεμον ἐόντα ξυνόν, καὶ δίκην ἔριν, καὶ γινόμενα πάντα κατ᾽ ἔριν καὶ χρεών.

γίγνομαι: become, come into being, be born, be produced

δέ: (Particle) but, but on the other hand, or just leave untranslated

δίκη, -ας, ἡ: justice, right, order, custom

ἔρις, -ιδος, ἡ: strife, quarrel, debate, contention, battle, fight, contest, disputation

καί: (Conj.) and, even, also

κατά: (+Acc.) according to, corresponding with, after the fashion of

κοινός, -ή, -όν: common, public, ordinary

πᾶς, πασα, πᾶν: all, every, each, whole

πόλεμος, -ου, ὁ: war, conflict, battle

χρεών, τό: necessity, fate, that which must be, that which is right, that which is expedient

χρή: (Impersonal + Inf.) it is necessary, one must, one ought, it must needs

εἰδέναι: Perf. Act. Inf. of οἶδα; translated in present tense

ἐόντα: Ionic. Acc Sg. of ὤν

ξυνός, -ή, -όν: Ionic form of κοινός, -ή, -όν

εἰδέναι...χρὴ...πόλεμον ἐόντα ξυνόν: Impersonal Construction + IS; *one must know that war is common*

καὶ δίκην ἔριν: Cont. IS; *and (that) justice is strife*

γινόμενα: Ionic Pres. Acc. Mid./Pass. part. of γίγνομαι

γινόμενα πάντα: *all things come to be/ come into being/become*

κατ᾽ ἔριν καὶ χρεών: κατά with both ἔριν and χρεών; *according to strife and necessity*

B 81 ἡ δὲ τῶν ῥητόρων εἰσαγωγή...κατὰ τὸν Ἡράκλειτον κοπίδων ἐστὶν ἀρχηγός.

ἀρχηγός, -ά, -όν: chief, prince, captain, lead
εἰσαγωγή, -ῆς, ὁ: introduction, guide
καί: (Conj.) and, even, also
κατά: (+Acc.) according to, corresponding with, after the fashion of

κόπις, -ιδος, ὁ: liar, wrangler, prater
πᾶς, πασα, πᾶν: all, every, each, whole
ῥήτωρ, -ορος, ὁ: orator, public speaker, rhetorician

ἡ...τῶν ῥητόρων εἰσαγωγή: Partitive Gen.;[xxxix] *the orators' introduction*
ἐστὶν ἀρχηγός: take ἀρχηγός as Pred. Adj. referring to εἰσαγωγή
κοπίδων...ἀρχηγός: Partitive Gen.[xl]

Notes:

- Although not cited in neither the fragment, nor its doxa, Robinson contends that Heraclitus may have had Pythagoras in mind, especially in light of B 40 and B 129 (although the DK treats B 129 as spurious)[xli]

B 82 πιθήκων ὁ κάλλιστος αἰσχρὸς ἀνθρώπων γένει συμβάλλειν.

αἰσχρός, -ά, -όν: shameful, dishonorable, reproachful, ugly, ill-favored, base, disgraceful
ἄνθρωπος, -ου, ὁ: man, human
γένος, -ους, τὸ: race, stock, kind, class, family, generation, sort, descent, kin

καλός, -ή, -όν: beautiful, noble, good, fair, genuine, honorable, virtuous, happy
πίθηκος, -ου, ὁ: ape, monkey, dwarf
συμβάλλω: conjecture, infer, conclude, interpret; *Literally*: to throw together (+Dat)

πιθήκων: Part. Gen. Pl.; *of apes*
(ἐστίν) αἰσχρὸς: *is shameful*
συμβάλλειν: Pres. Act. Inf. of συμβάλλω: take here as *to compare* (+Dat. γένει)

B 83 ἀνθρώπων ὁ σοφώτατος πρὸς θεὸν πίθηκος φανεῖται καὶ σοφίᾳ κάλλει καὶ τοῖς ἄλλοις πᾶσιν.

ἄλλος, -η, -ον: another, one besides; (w/Article) the rest, the others
ἀνθρώπος, -ου, ὁ: man, human
θεὸς, -οῦ, ὁ: deity, god, divine
κάλλος, -ους, τὸ: beauty, nobility, something or somebody beautiful
πᾶς, πασα, πᾶν: all, every, each, whole
πίθηκος, -ου, ὁ: ape, monkey, dwarf

πρὸς: (+Acc.) in propotion to, in relation to, in comparison with
σοφία, -ας, ἡ: wisdom, cleverness, skill, cunning, learning
σοφός, -ή, -όν: wise, clever, prudent, skillful, intelligent
φαίνω: (+ Pred. Adj.) appear, come into being, bring to light, shows, displays

ἀνθρώπων: (Part. Gen.) *of men*
φανεῖται: 3rd Fut. Mid. Contr. form of φαίνομαι
καὶ...καὶ: *both...and*
σοφίᾳ κάλλει: Dat. of Respect[xlii]; *in (reference to) wisdom and beauty*
κάλλει: Dat. Sg. of κάλλος; *in beauty*

B 84 μεταβάλλον ἀναπαύεται καὶ κάματός ἐστι τοῖς αὐτοῖς μοχθεῖν καὶ ἄρχεσθαι.

ἀναπαύω: to make to cease; stop; to hinder from a thing; rest; make something rest
ἄρχω: to rule, govern, command, be leader of; begin
αὐτός, -ή, -όν: (Art. + form of αὐτός, -ή, -όν) the same

κάματος, -ου, ὁ: toil, trouble, weariness, pain
μεταβάλλω: to turn about, alter, change
μοχθέω (-ῶ): to be weary, worn with toil, to be sore, to labor

μεταβάλλον: Pres. N. Part.; *changing*
τοῖς αὐτοῖς: Ambiguous Dat. here; could be M. or N. Dat. Pl.; *to/for the same*
ἄρχεσθαι: Pres. Mid./Pass. Inf.

B 85 θυμῷ μάχεσθαι χαλεπόν· ὅ τι γὰρ ἂν θέλῃ, ψυχῆς ὠνεῖται.

γάρ: (Conj.) for, since
ἐθέλω: will, want, wish
θυμός, -οῦ: spirit, desire, heart, passion
μάχομαι: to fight with (+Dat.), fight against (+Dat.)

χαλεπός, -ή, -όν: difficult, hard, grievous
ψυχή, -ῆς, ἡ: soul, spirit, mind, life, ghost
ὠνέομαι: to buy, purchase, bid for

χαλεπόν (ἐστίν): (*it is*) *difficult*
μάχεσθαι: Pres. Mid./Pas. Inf. of μάχομαι; *to fight* (+ Dat.)
ὅ τι: Sub. of θέλῃ
θέλῃ: 3rd Sg. Pres. Subj. Act. of ἐθέλω; *whatever it desires*
ψυχῆς ὠνεῖται: *it purchases (at the price of) the soul* OR *buys from the soul*
ὠνεῖται: 3rd Sg. Pres. Act. Ind. of ὠνέομαι

B 86 ἀλλὰ τῶν μὲν θείων τὰ πολλά, καθ᾽ Ἡράκλειτον, ἀπιστίη διαφυγγάνει μὴ γιγνώσκεσθαι.

ἀλλά: (Conj.) but
ἀπιστία, -ας, ἡ: unbelief, distrust, disbelief
γιγνώσκω: to know, perceive, understand, be aware of
διαφεύγω: (alt. form is διαφυγγάνω) to escape, get away from, escape one; notice
θεῖος, -α, -ον: of or from the gods, divine, sacred, holy

κατά: (Prep. +Acc.) according to; in, along, through, downwards
μή: (Particle) no, not
πολύς, πολλή, πολύ: (with nouns of mass/amount) a lot of, much, great amount; (pl.) many

ἀπιστίη: Dat. Sg. Ionic of ἀπιστία, *by disbelief*
διαφυγγάνει: 3rd Sg. Pres. Ind. of διαφεύγω; subj. is τὰ πολλά: *escape notice*; (Compound Verbs of φεύγω can take the Inf. with a redundant μη)[xliii]
γιγνώσκεσθαι: Pres. Mid./Pas. Inf. of γιγνώσκω

63

Β 87 βλὰξ ἄνθρωπος ἐπὶ παντὶ λόγῳ ἐπτοῆσθαι φιλεῖ.

ἄνθρωπος,-ου, ὁ: man, human, person
βλὰξ, βλάκος, ὁ, ἡ: stupid, soft, stolid
ἐπί: (+Dat.) at, on, upon, in
λόγος, -ου, ὁ: best to leave it as λόγος (or) as
word, account, reason, understanding

πᾶς, πασα, πᾶν: all, every, each, whole
πτοέω: to dismay, distract, excite, scare, terrify
φιλέω (-ῶ): to love, like, approve, to be fond of

    ἐπὶ παντὶ λόγῳ: *at any speech/account/λόγος*
    ἐπτοῆσθαι: Perf. Mid/Pas Inf. of πτοέω; Comp. Inf. of φιλεῖ; *to be excited/distracted*
    φιλεῖ: 3rd Ind. Sg. Pres. Act. of φιλέω

Β 88 ταὐτό τ᾽ ἔνι ζῶν καὶ τεθνηκὸς καὶ τὸ ἐγρηγορὸς καὶ τὸ κάθεῦδον καὶ νέον καὶ γηραιόν· τάδε γὰρ μεταπεζόντα ἐκεῖνά ἐστι κἀκεῖνα πάλιν μεταπεζόντα ταῦτα.

γάρ: (Conj.) for, since
γηραιός, -ά, -όν: old, aged
ἐγείρω: to awaken, rouse
ἐκεῖνος, ἐκείνη, ἐκεῖνο: (Dem. Pro.) that (Pl.)
those
εἷς, μία, ἕν: (Gen. ἑνός) one
ἐν: (Prep. + Dat.) in, on, at, among
ζάω (-ῶ): to live

καθεύδω: to sleep, lie sleep
καί: (Conj.) and, even, also
μεταπίπτω: to change in form, fall differently
νέος, -α, -ον: young, new
πάλιν: (Adv.) again, back
ὅδε, ἥδε, τόδε: (Dem.) this
οὗτος, αὕτη, τοῦτο: this; (Pl.) those, these
θνήσκω: to die, to be dying

    τεθνηκὸς... ἐγρηγορὸς: Part. Sg. Perf. Act. N. of θνήσκω and ἐγείρω
    κάθεῦδον: Part. Sg. Pres. Act. N. of καθεύδω
    τὸ ἐγρηγορὸς καὶ τὸ κάθεῦδον: Attrib. Part. as Substantives;[xliv] *the awakened and the asleep*
    ταὐτό: Crasis of τό αὐτόν
    μεταπεζόντα: Pl. N. Aor. Part. of μεταπίπτω
    κἀκεῖνα: Crasis of καί ἐκεῖνα

B 89 ὁ Ἡ. φησι τοῖς ἐγρηγορόσιν ἕνα καὶ κοινὸν κόσμον εἶναι, τῶν δὲ κοιμωμένων ἕκαστον εἰς ἴδιον ἀποστρέφεσθαι.

ἀποστρέφω: to turn back; to turn aside; to divert
ἐγρείρω: to awaken, rouse
εἷς, μία, ἕν: (Gen. ἑνός) one
ἕκαστος, -η, -ον: each, every
ἴδιος, -α, -ον: one's own, personal, private

καί: (Conj.) and, even, also
κοιμάω (ῶ): to sleep; (Mid./Pass.) to be put to sleep
κοινός, -ή, -όν: common, public, ordinary
κόσμος, -ου, ὁ: order, world, universe, earth

ὁ Ἡ. φησι... κοινὸν κόσμον εἶναι: IS; *Heraclitus says that there is...*
τοῖς ἐγρηγορόσιν: Attributive Perf. Act. Part.; *to/for those who are awakened*
τῶν δὲ κοιμωμένων: Mini. Gen. Abs.; *but with (many) being asleep*
ἀποστρέφεσθαι: Pres. Mid./Pass. Inf. of ἀποστρέφω; used as verb in
ἕκαστον εἰς ἴδιον ἀποστρέφεσθαι: cont. IS; *that each is turned into one's own (κόσμος)*

B 90 πυρός τε ἀνταμοιβὴ τὰ πάντα καὶ πῦρ ἁπάντων ὅκωσπερ χρυσοῦ χρήματα καὶ χρημάτων χρυσός.

ἀνταμοιβή, -ῆς, ἡ: interchange
ἅπας, ἅπασα, ἅπαν: all, the whole, everything
καί: (Conj.) and, even, also
ὅκωσπερ: (Conj.) just as, in such a manner as
πῦρ, πυρός, τό: fire; funeral-fire, sacrificial fire, hearthfire

πᾶς, πασα, πᾶν: all, every, each, whole
τε: (Conj.) and, also, but
χρῆμα, -ατος, τό: property, good, thing, matter
χρυσός, -οῦ, ὁ: gold coin, gold

τε...καὶ: Correl. Conj.; *both....and*
πυρός... τὰ πάντα...χρημάτων χρυσός: Gen. of Value[xlv] for each of the four Gen. and
  Noun pairs; *all things for fire...gold for property*

B 91 ποταμῷ γὰρ οὐκ ἔστιν ἐμβῆναι δὶς τῷ αὐτῷ καθ᾽ Ἡράκλειτον. οὐδὲ θνητῆς οὐσίας δὶς ἅψασθαι κατὰ ἕξιν· ἀλλ᾽ ὀξύτητι καὶ τάχει μεταβολῆς σκίδνησι καὶ πάλιν συνάγει καὶ πρόσεισι καὶ ἄπεισι.

ἀλλά: (Conj.) but
ἅπτω: (+ Gen.) to touch, affect, engage in
αὐτός, -ή, -όν: (Article + form of αὐτός, -ή, -όν) the same
ἀφίημι: to send forth, send away, let loose
γάρ: (Conj.) for, since
δὶς: (Adv.) twice, doubly
ἐμβαίνω: to step in
ἕξις, -εως, ἡ: state, habit
θνητός, -ή, -όν: mortal, human, mortal creature, one liable to death
καί: (Conj.) and, even, also
κατά: (Prep. +Acc.) in, along, through, downwards, according to

μεταβολη, -ῆς, ἡ: change, transformation
ὀξύτης, -ητος, ἡ: sharpness, pointedness
οὐδέ: (Conj.) and not, nor, but not
οὐκ: (Particle) no, not
οὐσία, -ας, ἡ: being, substance, essence, thinghood
πάλιν: (Adv.) again, back
ποταμός, -οῦ, ὁ: river, stream
πρόσειμι: to be present, to be at hand
σκίδνημι: to disperse, spread, scatter
συνάγω: to bring together, gather together
τάχος, -εος, τό: swiftness

ποταμῷ...τῷ αὐτῷ: *in the same river*
οὐκ ἔστιν: *it is not (possible)*
οὐδὲ: Nor (is it possible)
ἅψασθαι: Aor. Mid. Inf. of ἅπτω
κατὰ ἕξιν: *as far as its state*
σκίδνησι: 3rd Sg. Act. Pres. Ind. of σκίδνημι
ὀξύτητι καὶ τάχει: Dat. Sg.; *by the sharpness and swiftness*
καὶ πρόσεισι καὶ ἄπεισι: Both are 3rd Sg. Act. Pres. Act. Ind.; *it comes to be present and it goes away*

B 92 Σίβυλλα δὲ μαινομένῳ στόματι καθ᾽ Ἡράκλειτον ἀγέλαστα καὶ ἀκαλλώπιστα καὶ ἀμύριστα φθεγγομένη χιλίων ἐτῶν ἐξικνεῖται τῇ φωνῇ διὰ τὸν θεόν.

ἀγέλαστος, -η, -ον: grave, serious; (Lit.) not laughing
ἀκαλλώπιστος, -η, -ον: unadorned
ἀμύριστος, -η, -ον: rude, rough
διά: (Prep. + Acc.): through, on account of, because of, thanks to, by the aid of
ἐξικνέομαι: to arrive, reach, come to (someplace); to complete, accomplish
ἔτος, -εος, τό: year

θεός, οῦ, ὁ: god, deity
καί: (Conj.) and, even, also
μαίνομαι: to rave, rage, be mad, be angry
Σίβυλλα,-ας, ἡ: the Sibyl, prophetess
στόμα, -ατος, τό: mouth, face
φθέγγομαι: to utter, rave, shout loudly, cry out, proclaim
φωνή, -ῆς, ἡ: voice, speech, utterance, sound
χίλιοι, -αι, -α: (Pl.) thousand(s)

μαινομένῳ στόματι: Pres. Dat. Part.; *with a raging mouth*
ἐξικνεῖται: 3ʳᵈ Sg. Pres. Mid./Pas. of ἐξικνέομαι; *reaches out*
χιλίων ἐτῶν: Gen. of Time; *over the thousands of years*
φθεγγομένη: Pres. Nom. Mid./Pas. Part. of φθέγγομαι; *raving* +Acc. (ἀγέλαστα καὶ ἀκαλλώπιστα καὶ ἀμύριστα)

B 93 ὁ ἄναξ οὗ τὸ μαντεῖόν ἐστι τὸ ἐν Δελφοῖς, οὔτε λέγει οὔτε κρύπτει ἀλλὰ σημαίνει.

ἀλλά: (Conj.) but
ἄναξ, ἄνακτος, ὁ: lord, master, king
Δελφοί, -ῶν, οἱ: Delphi
ἐν: (Prep. + Dat.) in, on, at, among
κρύπτω: to hide, cover, conceal, keep secret

λέγω: say, speak, converse, tell a story
μαντεῖόν, τό: oracle, oracular response, seat of an oracle
οὔτε...οὔτε: (Correl.) neither...nor
σημαίνω: to indicate, show by a sign, point out, give a sign

οὗ μαντεῖόν ἐστιν τὸ: *whose oracle is the one*
λέγει...κρύπτει...σημαίνει: 3ʳᵈ Sg. Pres. Act. Ind. forms

B 94 ἥλιος γὰρ οὐχ ὑπερβήσεται μέτρα· εἰ δὲ μή, Ἐρινύες μιν Δίκης ἐπίκουροι ἐξευρήσουσιν.

Δίκη, Δίκης, ἡ: Dike, the goddess of justice, law, order, right, judgment
εἷς, μία, ἕν: (Gen. ἑνός) one
ἐξευρίσκω: to find out, seek out, discover, win, procure, get, search
ἐπίκουρος, ἐπικούρου, ὁ: ally, friend, protector, assistant, guard

Ἐρινύες: the Furies; the three Greek female gods of punishment, vengeance, and curses
ἥλιος, ἡλίου, ὁ: the sun, daylight, sunshine
μέτρον, -ου, τό: measure, rule, length, space, dimension
ὑπερβαίνω: to step over, transgress, go beyond, overstep, surpass

> **ὑπερβήσεται**: 3rd Sg. Fut. Mid. Ind. of ὑπερβαίνω
> **εἰ δὲ μή**: *and if not*
> **μιν**: Acc. Fem. Act. Sg. of μία
> **ἐξευρήσουσιν**: 3rd Pl. Fut. Act. Ind. of ἐξευρίσκω

B 95 ἀμαθίην γὰρ ἄμεινον κρύπτειν, ἔργον δὲ ἐν ἀνέσει καὶ παρ' οἶνον.

ἀγαθός, -ή, -όν: good, noble, brave, fortunate
ἄνεσις, -εως, ἡ: loosening, relaxing, indulgence
ἀμαθία, -ας, ἡ: ignorance, stupidity, boorishness
γάρ: (Conj,) for, since
δέ: (Particle) but, but on the other hand, or just leave untranslated
ἐν: (Prep. + Dat.) in, on, at, among

ἔργον, -ου, τό: deed, burden, action, labor, work
κρύπτω: to hide, cover, conceal, keep secret, suppress, lie hidden
οἶνος, -ου, ὁ: wine; or cup (presumably to hold wine)
παρά: (Prep. + Acc.) beside, over, along, beyond, near, by

> **ἀμαθίην γὰρ ἄμεινον κρύπτειν [Implied ἐστί]**: *it is better to conceal ignorance*
> **ἀνέσει**: Dat. Sg. of ἄνεσις
> **ἔργον δὲ ἐν ἀνέσει καὶ παρ' οἶνον**: (Presumably with preceding ἐστί) *but it (is) a labor (to conceal ignorance)...*

B 96 νέκυες γὰρ κοπρίων ἐκβλητότεροι.

γάρ: (Conj,) for, since	κόπριον, -ου, τό: dirt, filth
ἔκβλητος, -α, -ον: thrown out, cast overboard	νέκυς, νέκυος, ὁ: corpse, body

κοπρίων ἐκβλητότεροι: (Comp. + Gen. of Comparison; *more suited to be rejected/thrown out than dung*

Notes:

- Both Burnet and Robinson render ἐκβλητότεροι as either "more fit to be cast out" or "more worthy to be thrown out," respectively.
- The sentiment can be conveyed without having to make ἐκβλητότεροι into a pseudo-passive infinitive since Heraclitus is essentially claiming that corpses are of no greater worth than that of mere dung.

B 97 κύνες γὰρ καταβαΰζουσιν ὧν ἂν μὴ γινώσκωσι.

γιγνώσκω: to know, perceive, understand, be aware of	καταβαΰζω: to bark at, bark against
κατά: (Prep. +Acc.) in, along, through, downwards, according to	κύων, κυνός, ὁ or ἡ: dog (either male or female)
	μὴ: (Particle) no, not

ὧν: Gen. Pl. Rel. Pro.; Obj. of καταβαΰζουσιν; *bark at/against those whom*
ἂν: Not used here in conditional; used here to mark generality; untranslatable in English
γινώσκωσι: Alt. form for the 3rd Pl. Pres. Subj. of γιγνώσκω

B 98 αἱ ψυχαὶ ὀσμῶνται καθ᾿ Ἅιδην.

Ἅιδης, Ἅιδου, ὁ: Hades (referring either to the God of the underworld or the underworld itself)	ὀσμάομαι (ὦμαι): to have a sense of smell; smell
κατά: (Prep. +Acc.) in, along, through, downwards, according to	ψυχή, -ῆς, ἡ: soul, spirit, mind, life, ghost

ὀσμῶνται: 3rd Pl. Pres. Mid./Pas. Ind. of ὀσμάομαι

B 99 εἰ μὴ ἥλιος ἦν, ἕνεκα τῶν ἄλλων ἄστρων εὐφρόνη [ἄν] ἦν.

ἄλλος, -η, -ον: another, one besides; (w/Article) the rest, the others
ἄστρον, -ου, τό: a star
εἰ: (Conj.) if
ἕνεκα: (Prep. + Gen.) for the sake of, on account of, for, in consequence of, because

εὐφρόνη, -ης, ἡ: literally *the kindly time*; Euphemism for *night*
ἥλιος, - ου ὁ: sun
μή: (Particle) no, not

    εἰ... ἦν...[ἄν] ἦν: Pres. CTF conditional; *if the sun were not....would be*
    ἦν: 1st Sg. Impf. Act. Ind. of εἰμί
    ἕνεκα: Take this causally as *on account of/as a consequence of* (+Gen.)

B 100 περιόδους· ὧν ὁ ἥλιος ἐπιστάτης ὢν καὶ σκοπὸς ὁρίζειν καὶ βραβεύειν καὶ ἀναδεικνύναι καὶ ἀναφαίνειν μεταβολὰς καὶ ὥρας αἳ πάντα φέρουσι καθ᾽ Ἡράκλειτον.

ὅς, ἥ, ὅ: (Rel. Pro.) who, which
πᾶς, πασα, πᾶν: all, every, each, whole

φέρω: to bring, bear, offer, produce
ὥρα, -ας, ἡ: season, period, part of the year

    ὥρας: Acc. Pl. of ὥρα
    αἳ: Fem. Pl. Nom. Rel. Pro.

B 101 ἐδιζησάμην ἐμεωυτόν.

δίζημαι: to search for, seek, seek the meaning of, look for

ἐμαυτοῦ: (only in Gen., Dat., and Acc.) myself

    ἐδιζησάμην: 1st Sg. Imp. Mid. of δίζημαι
    ἐμεωυτόν: Ionic form of Acc. Sg. of ἐμαυτόν

B 102 τῷ μὲν θεῷ καλὰ πάντα καὶ ἀγαθὰ καὶ δίκαια, ἄνθρωποι δὲ ἅ μὲν ἄδικα ὑπειλήφασιν ἃ δὲ δίκαια.

ἀγαθός, -ή, -όν: good, noble, brave, fortunate
ἄδικος, -α, -ον: unjust, wrong, unrighteous
ἄνθρωπος,-ου, ὁ: man, human, person
δέ: (Particle) but, but on the other hand, or just leave untranslated
δίκαιος, -ία, -ιον: just, righteous, lawful, right

θεός, οῦ, ὁ: god, deity
καί: (Conj.) and, even, also
καλός, -ή, όν: (Adj.) good, beautiful, beauteous, fair, noble
μέν: (Particle) indeed
πᾶς, πασα, πᾶν: all, every, each, whole
ὑπολαμβάνω: to suppose, to assume, to suspect

τῷ μὲν θεῷ: Dat. Sg.[xlvi]; *to god*
μὲν...ἄνθρωποι δὲ: (Correl. Clauses) *on the one hand....on the other hand*
καλὰ πάντα καὶ ἀγαθὰ καὶ δίκαια: Implied (ἐστί); *all things are good, noble, and just*
ἄνθρωποι δὲ: *but men...*
ὑπειλήφασιν: 3rd Pl. Perf. Ind. Act. of ὑπολαμβάνω
ἅ μὲν... ἃ δὲ: N. Pl. Art. + Correl.; *some things....(and) other things*

B 103 ξυνὸν γὰρ ἀρχὴ καὶ πέρας ἐπὶ κύκλου περιφερείας

ἀρχή, -ῆς, ἡ: beginning, origin
ἐπὶ: (Prep.) (+ Gen.): on, upon, at
κοινός, -ή, -όν: common, public, ordinary

κύκλος, -ου, ὁ: circle, ring
πέρας, πέρατος, τό: limit, end, boundary
περιφέρεια, -ας, ἡ: circumference

ξυνὸν: Ionic form of κοινόν
ἀρχὴ καὶ πέρας (εἰσίν): *the beginning and the end (are)*

B 104 τίς γὰρ αὐτῶν νόος ἢ φρήν; δήμων ἀοιδοῖσι πείθονται καὶ διδασκάλῳ χρείωνται ὁμίλῳ οὐκ εἰδότες ὅτι οἱ πολλοὶ κακοί, ὀλίγοι δὲ ἀγαθοί.

ἀγαθός, -ή, -όν: good, noble, brave, fortunate
ἀοιδός, -οῦ, ὁ: bard, minstrel, singer
αὐτός, -ή, -όν: (Article + form of αὐτός, -ή, -όν) the same; or else reflexive
γάρ: (Conj.) for, since
δέ: (Particle) but, but on the other hand, or just leave untranslated
δῆμος, -ου, ὁ: people, populace
διδασκάλος, -ου, ὁ: teacher, master, trainer
ἤ: (Conj.) or
καί: (Conj.) and, even, also
κακός, -ή, όν: wicked, evil, mean, ugly, ignoble, base, baneful, bad

νοῦς, νοῦ, ὁ: mind intelligence, wit
οἶδα: (Perf. translated as Pres.) I know
ὀλίγος, -η, -ον: few, small, little
ὅμιλος, -ου, ὁ: crowd, throng, tumult
ὅτι: that
οὐκ: (Particle) no, not
πείθω: (Act.) persuade, convince; (Mid./Pas.) to obey, trust, believe (+ Dat.)
πολύς, πολλή, πολύ: (with nouns of mass/amount) a lot of, much, great amount; many
τίς, τίς, τί: (Interrogative Pro.) who? what?
φρήν, φρενός, ἡ: heart, mind, imagination
χράομαι: to use, regard, treat (+ Dat.)

νόος: Ionic form of νοῦς
χρείωνται: 3rd Pl. Pres. Dep. of χράομαι
διδασκάλῳ χρείωνται ὁμίλῳ: *they regard* (+Dat.) *the crowd (as its) teacher*
εἰδότες: Part. Pl. Perf. of οἶδα; *having known*
πολλοὶ κακοί ὀλίγοι δὲ ἀγαθοί: Implied εἰσί for both phrases

B 105 Ἡ. ἐντεῦθεν ἀστρολόγον φησὶ τὸν Ὅμηρον...ἔμμεναι

ἀστρολόγος, -ου, ὁ: someone who studies the stars or astronomy
ἐντεῦθεν: (Adv.) hence, from here, hence; from this time, henceforth

Ὅμηρος, -ου, ὁ: Homer
φημί: to say, speak, agree

ἔμμεναι: Epic. Pres. Inf. of εἰμί
Ἡ...φησὶ τὸν Ὅμηρον...ἔμμεναι: IS; *Heraclitus says that Homer*

72

B 106 unus diēs pār omnī est.

---

diēs, - ēī, m./f.: day
omnis, -is, -e: every, each; (pl.) all

pār: (M./F./N. Adj.) equal, like, even, suitable
unus, -a, um: one

pār omnī: (Dat. with Adj. pār); *...equal to each/every (day)*

B 107 κακοὶ μάρτυρες ἀνθρώποισιν ὀφθαλμοὶ καὶ ὦτα βαρβάρους ψυχὰς ἐχόντων.

ἀνθρώπος, -ου, ὁ: man, human
βαρβάρος, -α, -ον: foreign, non-Greek, barbarian
ἔχω: to have, hold, possess
κακός, -ή, όν: wicked, evil, mean, ugly, ignoble, base, baneful, bad

μάρτυς, μάρτυρος, ἡ or ὁ: witness
οὖς, ὠτός, τό: ear
ὀφθαλμός, -οῦ, ὁ: eye
ψυχή: soul, spirit, vital spirit, animating principle, ghost

ὦτα: Nom. Pl. of οὖς
ἀνθρώποισιν: Dat. of Reference[xlvii]; *to/for men*
ἐχόντων: Circum. Pres. Gen. Pl. Act. Part. of ἔχω in Gen. Abs. w/other noun implied by context[xlviii]; *of those having* + Acc. (βαρβάρους ψυχὰς)

73

B 108 ὁκόσων λόγους ἤκουσα, οὐδεὶς ἀφικνεῖται ἐς τοῦτο, ὥστε γινώσκειν ὅτι σοφόν ἐστι πάντων κεχωρισμένον.

ἀκούω: to hear something (Acc.); to hear from/of someone (+Gen.)
ἀφικνέομαι: to arrive, reach
γιγνώσκω: to know, perceive, understand, be aware of
εἰς: (Prep + Acc.) into, onto, up to, until
λόγος, -ου, ὁ: best to leave it as λόγος (or) as word, account, reason, understanding
ὅστις, ἥτις, ὅτι: whoever, anyone, anything

ὁπόσος, -η, -ον: as many as, as much as; (In IQ) however much, however many
ὅστις, ἥτις, ὅτι: whoever, anyone, anything
οὐδείς, οὐδεμία, οὐδέν: no one, nothing
πᾶς, πασα, πᾶν: all, every, each, whole
σοφός, -ή, -όν: wise, prudent, skilled, clever, learned, ingenious, cleverly devised
οὗτος, αὕτη, τοῦτο: this; (Pl.) those, these
ὥστε: (Adv.) so as, as being, inasmuch as
χωρίζω: to separate, divide, distinguish

ὁκόσων: Gen. Pl. Ionic of ὁπόσος
ἤκουσα: 1st Sg. Aor. Act. Ind. of ἀκούω
ἐς: = εἰς
κεχωρισμένον: Perf. Mid./Pas. Part. of χωρίζω; antecedent is ὅτι σοφόν
ἀφικνεῖται: 3rd Sg. Pres. Mid./Pass. of ἀφικνέομαι
ὥστε γινώσκειν: Natural Result Clause; *so as/in order to know*

B 109 κρύπτειν ἀμαθίην κρέσσον ἢ ἐς τὸ μέσον φέρειν.

ἀμαθία, -ας, ἡ: ignorance, stupidity, boorishness
εἰς: (Prep + Acc.) into, onto, up to, until
κρύπτω: to hide, cover, conceal, keep secret, suppress, lie hidden

μέσος, -η, -ον: middle, midst, intervening space
φέρω: to bring, bear, convey, produce, bring forward

ἀμαθίην: Ionic, Acc. Sg. form of ἀμαθία
κρέσσον: N. Sg. Ionic form of κρείττων; Comp. form of κρατύς; *it is better*
κρέσσον ἢ: (Comp. + ἢ) *better than*
ἐς: εἰς
ἐς τὸ μέσον: with the preceding article τό, take μέσον substantively as *into the open* or *into the intervening space*

74

B 110 ἀνθρώποις γίνεσθαι ὁκόσα θέλουσιν οὐκ ἄμεινον

ἀγαθός, -ή, -όν: good, noble, brave, fortunate
ἄνθρωπος, -ου, ὁ: man, human
γίγνομαι: become, come into being, be born, be produced

ἐθέλω: will, want, wish
ὁπόσος, -η, -ον: as many as, as much as; (In IQ) however much, however many
οὐκ: (Particle) no, not

ὁκόσα: Ionic Neuter Pl. form of ὁπόσος, -η, -ον;
θέλουσιν: 3ʳᵈ Pl. Pres. Delib. Subj. after an IQ[xlix]
ἄμεινον: Neuter Irreg. Comp. of ἀγαθός, -ή, -όν
ἀνθρώποις...οὐκ ἄνεινον (ἐστί): take here as *for men...it is not better*

B 111 νοῦσος ὑγιείην ἐποίησεν ἡδύ, κακὸν ἀγαθόν, λιμὸς κόρον, κάματος ἀνάπαυσιν.

ἀγαθός, -ή, -όν: good
ἀνάπαυσις, ἀναπαύσεως, ἡ: rest, relaxation, relaxation
ἡδύς, ἡδεῖα, ἡδύ: sweet, pleasant, glad, well-pleased
κακός, -ή, όν: wicked, evil, mean, ugly, ignoble, base, baneful, bad
κάματος, καμάτου, ὁ: weariness, exhaustion, fatigue.

κόρος, -ου, ὁ: satisfaction, satiety, excess, abundance
λιμός, -οῦ, ὁ: hunger, famine
νόσος, -ου, ἡ: illness, sickness, plague, disease, suffering, madness, distress, bane
ποιέω (-ῶ): make, do, act, produce, cause
ὑγίεια, ὑγιείας, ἡ: health

νοῦσος: Ionic Sg. Nom. of νόσος
ὑγιείην: Ionic, Acc., Sg. of ὑγίεια
ἐποίησεν: 3ʳᵈ Sg. Act. Aor. of ποιέω

B 112 τὸ φρονεῖν ἀρετὴ μεγίστη, καὶ σοφίη ἀληθέα λέγειν καὶ ποιεῖν κατὰ φύσιν ἐπαΐοντας.

ἀληθής, -ές: true
ἀρετὴ, -ῆς, ἡ: virtue, goodness, excellence, merit
ἐπαΐω: to understand; to perceive/feel; to listen to
λέγω: say, speak, converse, tell a story

μέγας, μεγάλη, μέγα: big, great, vast, mighty, strong, important
σοφία, -ας, ἡ: wisdom, cleverness, skill, cunning, learning
φρονέω (ῶ): to think, to be wise, to understand, thinking well, being prudent

μεγίστη: Superl. of μεγάλη; modifies ἀρετὴ
τὸ φρονεῖν: N. Articular Inf.: *being wise, thinking*
σοφίη: Ionic Sg. Nom. form of σοφία
σοφίη ἀληθέα (ἐστί) λέγειν καὶ ποιεῖν: *true wisdom (is) to speak and to do*
κατὰ φύσιν: *according to nature*
ἐπαΐοντας: Pres. Pl. Acc. Part. of ἐπαΐω; *understanding/listening*

B 113 ξυνόν ἐστι πᾶσι τὸ φρονέειν.

κοινός, -ή, -όν: common, public, ordinary
πᾶς, πασα, πᾶν: all, every, each, whole

φρονέω (ῶ): to think, to be wise, to understand

ξυνόν: Ionic form of κοινόν; agrees with the N. Articular Inf. τὸ φρονέειν; AI can be treated like ordinary nouns in Greek
πᾶσι: Dat. Pl. Masc./Neut. of πᾶς or πᾶν; *to all*
τὸ φρονέειν: N. AI; *understanding*

B 114 ξὺν νόῳ λέγοντας ἰσχυρίζεσθαι χρὴ τῷ ξυνῷ πάντων, ὅκωσπερ νόμῳ πόλις, καὶ πολὺ ἰσχυροτέρως. τρέφονται γὰρ πάντες οἱ ἀνθρώπειοι νόμοι ὑπὸ ἑνὸς τοῦ θείου· κρατεῖ γὰρ τοσοῦτον ὁκόσον ἐθέλει καὶ ἐξαρκεῖ πᾶσι καὶ περιγίνεται.

ἀνθρώπειος, -α, -ον: human
γάρ: (Conj.) for, since
ἐθέλω: to will, want, wish
εἷς, μία, ἕν: (Gen. ἑνός) one
ἐξαρκέω: to suffice, be enough for
θεῖος, -α, -ον: of or from the gods, divine, sacred, holy
ἰσχυρίζομαι: to rely on, put trust in (something)
ἰσχυρός, -ά, -όν: strong, powerful
καί: (Conj.) and, even, also
κοινός, -ή, -όν: common, public, ordinary
κρατέω (ῶ): to rule, hold sway,
λέγω: say, speak, converse, tell a story
νόμος, -ου, ὁ: custom, law, ordinance
νόος, νόου, ὁ: intelligence, intellect, mind, sense, wit, reason, thought

ὅκωσπερ: just as, as
ὁπόσος, -η, -ον: as many as, as much as; (In IQ) however much, however many
πᾶς, πασα, πᾶν: all, every, each, whole
περιγίγνομαι: to be left over, to remain
πόλις, -εως, ἡ: polis, city-state
πολύς, πολλή, πολύ: (with nouns of mass/amount) a lot of, much, great amount; many
σύν: (Prep. + Dat.) with
τοσοῦτος, τοσαύτη, τοσοῦτο: so large, so many, so much
τρέφω: to nourish, feed, sustain
ὑπό: (Prep. + Gen. of Cause/Agent) by
χρή: (Impersonal +Inf.) it is necessary, one must, one ought, it must needs

νόῳ: Dat. Sg. of νόος
ξύν: Alt. form of σύν
ξυνῷ: Ionic form of κοινῷ
ἰσχυρίζεσθαι: Pres. Mid./Pas. Inf.
ἰσχυρίζεσθαι... τῷ ξυνῷ πάντων: *to hold fast to the common (part) of all things*
ὅκωσπερ νόμῳ πόλις: *just as a city (holds fast to its own) law*
ἰσχυροτέρως: Adv. of ἰσχυρός; *strongly*
τρέφονται: 3rd Pl. Pres. Mid. Ind. of τρέφω; *πάντες οἱ ἀνθρώπειοι νόμοι are nourished*
κρατεῖ γὰρ τοσοῦτον ὁκόσον: *for it (divine law) holds sway however much it wishes...*
καὶ ἐξαρκεῖ πᾶσι: *and it suffices for all*

B 115 ψυχῆς ἐστι λόγος ἑαυτὸν αὔξων.

αὐξάνω: to increase, strengthen, grow, promote
αὐτός, -ή, -όν: (Article + form of αὐτός, -ή, -όν) the same; or else reflexive

λόγος, -ου, ὁ: best to leave it as λόγος (or) as word, account, reason, understanding
ψυχή: soul, spirit, vital spirit, animating principle, ghost

αὔξων: Alt. form of αὐξάνων (Pres. Nom. Sg. Part. of αὐξάνω): *increasing, growing,*
ψυχῆς...λόγος: *λόγος of the soul*

B 116 ἀνθρώποισι πᾶσι μέτεστι γινώσκειν ἑωυτοὺς καὶ φρονεῖν.

γιγνώσκω: to know, perceive, understand, be aware of

ἑαυτοῦ, -ῆς, -οῦ: (No Nom.) himself, herself, itself

μέτειμι: to be among (L*it:* "to be with"); to have a part in, or to have a share in

πᾶς, πασα, πᾶν: all, every, each, whole

φρονέω (ὦ): to think, to have understanding, be wise, be prudent

μέτεστι: 3ʳᵈ Sg. Pres. Act. Ind. of μέτειμι; *are a part of* or *have a share in* (+ἀνθρώποισι πᾶσι)

γινώσκειν: Pres. Act. (Ionic) of γιγνώσκω

γινώσκειν...καὶ φρονεῖν: Compound Sub. of μέτεστι

ἑωυτοὺς: Ionic, Acc. Pl. form of ἑαυτοῦ, -ῆς, -οῦ; *themselves*

B 117 ἀνὴρ ὁκόταν μεθυσθῇ, ἄγεται ὑπὸ παιδὸς ἀνήβου σφαλλόμενος, οὐκ ἐπαίων ὅκη βαίνει, ὑγρήν τὴν ψυχὴν ἔχων.

ἄγω: to lead, lead towards a point, lead on, guide

ἀνήβος, -η, -ον: immature, prepubescent, young, childish

ἀνήρ, ἀνδρός, ὁ: man, male

βαίνω: to walk, step, go, set out

ἐπαίω: to have knowledge of, understand, perceive

ἔχω: to have, hold

μεθύσκω: to be drunk, to be intoxicated

ὁκόταν: (Adv.) whenever, whensoever (+Subj.)

ὅπη: (Adv.) wherever, in any direction/manner, by what way

οὐκ: (Particle) not, non

παῖς, παιδός, ὁ/ἡ: child, kid, son, daughter, boy, girl

σφάλλω: (when describing drunken behavior) to reel, to stagger

ὑγρός, - ά, -όν: wet, moist, fluid

ὑπό: (Prep. + Gen. of Cause/Agent) by

ψυχή, -ῆς, ἡ: spirit, soul, life, ghost

ὁκόταν: Ionic form of ὁπόταν

μεθυσθῇ: 3ʳᵈ Sg. Aor. Act. Subj. of μεθύσκω

σφαλλόμενος: Pres. Gen. Sg. Mid./Pas. Part. of σφάλλω; Antecedent is ἀνήρ; *he is led while staggering*

ὅκη: Ionic form of ὅπη

ὑγρήν τὴν ψυχὴν ἔχων: Antecedent is ἀνήρ; *having a wet soul*

78

B 118 αὐγὴ ξηρὴ ψυχὴ σοφωτάτη καὶ ἀρίστη

αὐγή, -ῆς, ἡ: light of the sun, sunlight, ray, gleam, sheen
ξηρός, -ή, -όν: dry, withered, lean

σοφός, -ή, -όν: wise, prudent, skilled, clever, learned, ingenious, cleverly devised
ψυχή, -ῆς, ἡ: spirit, soul, life, ghost

αὐγὴ [ἐστί] ξηρὴ ψυχὴ: *the light of the sun [is] the dry soul*
ἀρίστη: Fem. Sg. Superl. of ἀγαθός; agrees with αὐγή; *best*
σοφωτάτη: Fem. Sg. Superl. of σοφός; agrees with αὐγή; *wisest*

B 119 ἦθος ἀνθρώπῳ δαίμων.

ἀνθρώπος, -ου, ὁ: man, human
δαίμων, -ονος, ὁ/ἡ: god/goddess; LSJ takes this also as "the power controlling destiny of individuals: hence, one's *lot* or *fortune*;"

ἦθος, -ους, τό: disposition, character

ἀνθρώπῳ: Dative of Possession[l]: *The character (ἦθος) for a man (ἀνθρώπῳ)*

B 120 ἠοῦς καὶ ἑσπέρας τέρματα ἡ ἄρκτος καὶ ἀντίον τῆς ἄρκτου οὖρος αἰθρίου Διός.

αἰθρίος, -α, -ον: clear, bright
ἀντίος, -ία, ίον: opposite, contrary, set against; (+ Gen.) set against, opposite
ἄρκτος, -ου, ἡ: bear; the north; also refers to *Ursa Major*, the constellation
ἑσπέρα, -ας, ἡ: evening; the west
Ζεύς, Διός, ὁ: the god Zeus

ἠώς, ἠοῦς, ἡ: dawn, daybreak; the goddess of dawn, aurora
καί: (Conj.) and, even, also
ὅρος, -ου, ὁ: boundary, limit, frontier
οὖρος, οὔρου, ὁ: guardian, watcher
τέρμα, -ατος, τό: end, boundary, limit

ἀντίον τῆς ἄρκτου: *opposite the bear*
οὖρος: Burnett takes this as *boundary*[li]

B 121 ἄξιον Ἐφεσίοις ἡβηδὸν ἀπάγξασθαι <πᾶσι καὶ τοῖς ἀνήβοις τὴν πόλιν καταλιπεῖν>, οἵτινες Ἑρμόδωρον ἄνδρα ἑωυτῶν ὀνήιστον ἐξέβαλον φάντες· ἡμέων μηδὲ εἷς ὀνήιστος ἔστω, εἰ δὲ μή, ἄλλη τε καὶ μετ᾽ ἄλλων.

ἄλλος, -η, -ον: another, one besides; (w/ Art.) the rest, the others
ἀνήρ, ἀνδρός, ὁ: man
ἄνηβος, -ον: adolescent, pubescent
ἄξιος, -ία, -ιον: worthy, deserving to be
ἀπάγχω: to strangle, choke, hang
δέ: (Particle) but, but on the other hand, or just leave untranslated
εἰ: (Conj.) if
εἷς, μία, ἕν: (Gen. ἑνός) one
ἐκβάλλω: to throw out, banish, drive out
Ἑρμόδωρος, -ου, ὁ: Hermodorus
Ἐφεσίος, -α, -ον: Ephesian
ἑαυτοῦ, -ῆς, -οῦ: (No Nominative) himself, herself, itself

ἡβηδόν: (Adv.) from the youth up
ἡμεῖς: (Pro.) we
καί: (Conj.) and, even, also
καταλείπω: to leave behind, forsake, abandon, leave alone
μετά: (Prep. + Gen.) with, among, between
μή: (Particle) no, not
μηδὲ: (Conj.) and not
ὅστις, ἥτις, ὅτι: whoever, anyone, anything
ὄνειος, -α, -ον: valuable, useful
πᾶς, πασα, πᾶν: all, every, each, whole
πόλις, -εως, ἡ: polis, city-state
φημί: to say, speak, agree

ἄξιον Ἐφεσίοις: *it is worthy for (the) Ephesians*
ἀπάγξασθαι: Aor. Mid. Inf. of ἀπάγχω; *to be hanged/strangled*
τοῖς ἀνήβοις: Dat. of the Possessor[liii]; implied ἄξιον; *and (it is worthy) to the adolescents*
καταλιπεῖν: Pres. Act. Inf. of καταλείπω; τὴν πόλιν is its Obj.
οἵτινες: *whoever*
ἄνδρα ἑωυτῶν ὀνήιστον ἐξέβαλον: *threw out the strongest man among themselves*
ἡμέων: Ionic Gen. Pl. of ἡμεῖς
ἔστω: 3rd Sg. Pres. Imp.; μηδὲ...ἔστω; *and let there not be*
φάντες: Nom. Pl. Part. of φημί
ὀνήιστος: Ionic Superl. of ὄνειος; *most valuable*; ἑωυτῶν ὀνήιστον; *the most valuable among themselves*[liii]

Note:

- **Hermodorus**: The specific Hermodorus whom Heraclitus is referencing is relatively difficult to trace; Diogenes Laertius (*Lives and Opinions of the Eminent Philosophers*, IX.2) recounts that Hermodorus was simply Heraclitus' friend (ἑταῖρος)
- Bywater provides a list of the extant references to this fragment, but none seem to shed light on Hermodorus himself.[liv]

B 122 ἀγχιβατεῖν / ἀμφισβατεῖν : ἀγχιβασίην Ἡράκλειτος.

ἀγχιβασίη: (Lit.) stepping-near
ἀγχιβατέω (ῶ): (Lit.) to tread near

ἀμφισβατέω (ῶ): to dispute with

Notes:

- Out of all the fragments, this one is perhaps the most incomplete; Burnet just leaves this as "Debate."[lv]
- The Diels-Kranz notes provides the footnote "Annäherung" or "Approximation" on this fragment.
- Kirk, Raven, and Schofield contend that this fragment, cited in Sextus Empiricus' *Adversos Mathematicos,* compared the soul's resuscitation when brought near the λόγος, much like an ember reigniting when near a fire, hence the use of "ἀγχιβασίη" meaning "stepping-near."[lvi]
- Kahn contends that, despite the textual uncertainty of the work, there is no other reason to doubt this fragment's authenticity.[lvii]

B 123 φύσις δὲ καθ᾽ Ἡράκλειτον κρύπτεσθαι φιλεῖ.

δὲ: (Particle) but, and
κατά: (+Acc.) according to, corresponding with, after the fashion of
κρύπτω: to hide, cover, conceal, keep secret, suppress, lie hidden

φιλέω (-ῶ): to love, like, approve, to be fond of
φύσις, φύσεως, ἡ: nature, origin, birth, shape, form, kind

καθ᾽ Ἡράκλειτον: *according to Heraclitus*
κρύπτεσθαι: Pres. Mid./Pas. Inf. of κρύπτω; *to hide itself*

B 124 σάρμα εἰκῆ κεχυμένον ὁ κάλλιστος, φησὶν Ἡράκλειτος, [ὁ] κόσμος.

ἔοικα: to be like, seem
καλός, -ή, -όν: beautiful, noble, good, fair, genuine, honorable, virtuous, happy

κόσμος, -ου, ὁ: order, world, universe, earth
σάρμα, -ατος, τό: refuse pile, sweepings
χέω: to pour, scatter, shed, drop

εἰκῆ: 3rd Sg. Plup. Act. Ind. but Pres. in sense; *is*
κεχυμένον: Perf. Sg. N. Mid./Pas. of χέω; antecedent is σάρμα

81

B 125 καὶ ὁ κυκεὼν διίσταται <μὴ> κινούμενος.

διίστημι: to set apart, separate, stand apart
καί: (Conj.) and, even, also
κινέω (ῶ): to set in motion; (Pass./Mid.) to be
stirred/moved

κυκάω (ῶ): to stir, mix, confound
μή: (Particle) no, not

κυκεὼν: Pres. Nom. Sg. Act. Ionic Part. of κυκάω
διίσταται: 3rd Sg. Pres. Mid/Pas. Ind.
<μὴ> κινούμενος: μη + Part. indicates condition needed for an action to occur[lviii]; *if (it) is not
stirred*
κινούμενος: Pres. Nom. Sg. Mid/Pas Part. of κινέω

B 126 τὰ ψυχρὰ θέρεται, θερμὸν ψύχεται, ὑγρὸν αὐαίνεται, καρφαλέον νοτίζεται.

αὐαίνω: to dry, wither, waste away
θερμός, -ά, -όν: hot, warm, fresh
θέρω: to heat, make hot, make (+Acc. Obj.) warm
καρφαλέος, -α, -ον: dry, parched

νοτίζω: to moisten, to water; (Intrans.) to be wet
ὑγρός, -ά, -όν: wet, moist, fluid
ψυχρός, -ά, -όν: cold
ψύχω: to cool, make cold, make cool

τὰ ψυχρὰ θέρεται: N. Pl. takes Sg. Verb; *the cold things are made hot*
θέρεται...νοτίζεται...αὐαίνεται... νοτίζεται: 3rd Sg. Pres. Ind. Mid./Pas.

ENDNOTES

[i] Friedrich Schlegel, *Philosophical Fragments*, trans. Peter Firchow (University of Minnesota Press: Minneapolis, MN, 1991), 9.

[ii] Diogenes Laertius, *Lives of the Eminent Philosophers* IX.5.

[iii] Graham, Daniel W., "Heraclitus", *The Stanford Encyclopedia of Philosophy* (Summer 2021 Edition), Edward N. Zalta (ed.), URL = <https://plato.stanford.edu/archives/sum2021/entries/heraclitus/>.

[iv] G.W.F. Hegel, *Lectures on the History of Philosophy*, trans. Elizabeth Sanderson Haldane and Frances H Simson (London: Routledge and Paul, 1968), 166-67.

[v] *Ibid.*, 160.

[vi] Friedrich Nietzsche, *Philosophy and Truth : Selections from Nietzsche's Notebooks of the Early 1870's*, trans. Daniel Breazeale (New Jersey: Humanities Press, 1979), §53.

[vii] Friedrich Nietzsche, *Philosophy and Truth: Selections from Nietzsche's Notebooks of the Early 1870's*, trans. Daniel Breazeale (New Jersey: Humanities Press, 1979), §53.

[viii] Martin Heidegger, *Introduction to Metaphysics*, Second Edition, trans. Richard Polt and Gregory Fried (New Haven, CT: Yale University Press, 2014), 139.

[ix] See Smyth 2089c

[x] G.S. Kirk, J.E. Raven, and M. Schofield, *The Presocratic Philosophers*, Second Edition (Cambridge: Cambridge University Press, 1983), 187

[xi] See Smyth §1507.

[xii] See Smyth §1507.

[xiii] See Smyth §1606-08.

[xiv] See Smyth §1848.

[xv] See Smyth §1786.

[xvi] See Smyth §1831.

[xvii] See Smyth §2070.

[xviii] See Smyth §2000 on "Infinitives after Other Verbs"

[xix] See Smyth §2070.

[xx] See Smyth §1306 & §1307

[xxi] See Smyth §2458-59.

[xxii] See Smyth §2066.

[xxiii] See Diogenes Laertius, *Lives of the Eminent Philosophers,* Book IX,

[xxiv] Bywater, *The Fragments of the Work of Heraclitus of Ephesus on Nature*, trans. by G.T.W. Patrick (Baltimore, MD: N. Murray, 1889) 115.

[xxv] *Ibid.,* 115.

[xxvi] *Ibid.,* 115.

[xxvii] *Ibid.,* 115.

[xxviii] Charles Kahn, *The Art and Thought of Heraclitus* (Cambridge: Cambridge University Press, 1979) 54.

[xxix] G.S. Kirk, J.E. Raven, and M. Schofield, *The Presocratic Philosophers*, Second Edition (Cambridge: Cambridge University Press, 1983), 203.

[xxx] See Smyth §1361

[xxxi] See Smyth §1496

[xxxii] See Smyth 2049

[xxxiii] Wheelwright, Fragment 30

[xxxiv] T.M. Robinson, *Heraclitus: Fragments : A Text and Translation with a Commentary* (Toronto: University of Toronto Press, 1987), x.

[xxxv] Charles Kahn, *The Art and Thought of Heraclitus* (Cambridge: Cambridge University Press, 1979) 288.

[xxxvi] *Ibid.*

[xxxvii] Freeman, Kathleen, *Ancilla to the Pre-Scratic Philosophers a Complete Translation of the Fragment in Diels Fragmente der Vorsokratiker* (Cambridge, MA: Harvard Univ. Press, 1948) 34.

[xxxviii] See Smyth §1496

[xxxix] See Smyth §1306 & §1307

[xl] See Smyth §1312 & §1313

[xli] T.M. Robinson, *Heraclitus: Fragments : A Text and Translation with a Commentary* (Toronto: University of Toronto Press, 1987), 132-33.

[xlii] See Smyth §1516

[xliii] See Smyth 2750

[xliv] See Smyth §2052

[xlv] See Smyth §1372

[xlvi] See Smyth, §1459

[xlvii] See Smyth §1496

[xlviii] See Smyth §2072

[xlix] See Smyth §2677.

[l] See Smyth §1476

[li] John Burnet, *Early Greek Philosophy* (London: A & C Black, 1920) 105. https://www.plato.spbu.ru/RESEARCH/burnet/burnet.pdf

[lii] See Smyth §1476

[liii] See Smyth §1434.

[liv] Bywater, *The Fragments of the Work of Heraclitus of Ephesus on Nature*, trans. by G.T.W. Patrick (Baltimore, MD: N. Murray, 1889) 110.

[lv] Burnet, *Early Greek Philosophy*, 105.

[lvi] G.S. Kirk, J.E. Raven, and M. Schofield, *The Presocratic Philosophers*, Second Edition (Cambridge: Cambridge University Press, 1983), 206.

[lvii] Charles Kahn, *The Art and Thought of Heraclitus* (Cambridge: Cambridge University Press, 1979) 288.

[lviii] See Smyth §2731.

ALPHABETIZED DICTIONARY

-πεϱ: (Enclitic particle; added to end of a word) untranslatable but adds force and emphasis
ἀγαθός, -ή, -όν: good, noble, brave, fortunate
ἄγαλμα, -ατος, τό: image, sign; statue of a god; object of worship; gift
ἀγέλαστος, -η, -ον: grave, serious; (Lit.) not laughing
ἀγένητος, -η, -ον: un-generated, uncreated
ἀγχιβασίη: (Literally) stepping-near
ἀγχιβατέω (ῶ): (Literally) to tread near
ἄγω: to lead, lead towards a point, lead on, guide
ἀγών, -ῶνος, ὁ: gathering, assembly
ἄδικος, -α, -ον: unjust, wrong, unrighteous
ἀεί: (ADV.) always, ever
ἀείζωος, -ον: ever-living, everlasting; Compound of ἀεί and ζωός, -ά, -όν
ἀέναος, -α, -ον: ever-flowing, everlasting
ἀήϱ, ἀέϱος, ὁ: air
ἀθάνατος, -η, -ον: immortal, undying, everlasting, perpetual
ἄθυϱμα, ἀθύϱματος, τό: toy, plaything, adornment, delighy
Ἄιδης, Ἄιδου, ὁ: Hades (referring either to the God of the underworld or the underworld itself)
αἰδοῖον, -ίου, τό: genitals (whether male or female)
αἰθϱίος, -α, -ον: clear, bright
αἱμάς, -άδος, ἡ: blood, stream of blood
αἱϱέω: (Act.) take, seize, grasp; (Mid.) prefer, select, choose
ἆισμα, -ατος, τό: song, ode, hymn
αἰσχϱός, -ά, -όν: shameful, dishonorable, reproachful, ugly, ill-favored, base, disgraceful
αἰών, αἰῶνος, ὁ: time, epoch, eternity
ἀκαλλώπιστος, -η, -ον: unadorned
ἀκοὴ , -ῆς, -ἡ: hearing, listening; something heard, hearsay
ἄκος, -εος, τό: cure, remedy
ἀκούω: to hear something (Acc.); to hear from/of someone (+Gen.)
ἀλλά: (Conj.) but
ἀλλαχοῦ: (Adv.) elsewhere
ἀλλοιόω: to change, alter
ἄλλος, -η, -ον: another, one besides; (w/Article) the rest, the others
ἄλλως: (Adv.) otherwise, differently, generally
ἀμαθία, -ας, ἡ: ignorance, stupidity, boorishness
ἀμφισβατέω (ῶ): to dispute with
ἄν: (Particle) used to indicate limitation or mode; used in conditionals; marks an indefinite; (w/ no Protasis) expresses what might have occurred in the past
ἀναιδής, -ές: shameless, ruthless
ἄναξ, ἄνακτος, ὁ: lord, master, king
ἀνάπαυσις, ἀναπαύσεως, ἡ: rest, relaxation, relaxation
ἀναπαύω: (Mid./Pass.) to take rest; take one's sleep
ἀνέλπιστος, -ον: unhoped for, hopeless, unexpected
ἀνεξερεύνητος, -ον: not to be searched out, unsearched, uninvestigated
ἀνήβος, -η, -ον: immature, prepubescent, young, childish; adolescent, pubescent
ἀνήϱ, ἀνδϱός, ὁ: man
ἀνθρώπειος, -α, -ον: of or belonging to a human, human, suited to man, within man's powers
ἀνθρώπος, -ου, ὁ: man, human
ἀμαθία, -ας, ἡ: ignorance, stupidity, boorishness
ἄνεσις, -εως, ἡ: loosening, relaxing, indulgence
ἀμύϱιστος, -η, -ον: rude, rough
ἀνίεϱος, -η, -ον: impious, unholy, profane, sacrilegious

ἀνταμοιβὴ, -ῆς, ἡ: interchange
ἀντί-εἰμι: to go opposite, come opposite to
ἀντὶ: (Prep. + Gen.) instead of, in the place of, over against, opposite, in return for
ἀντίξοος, -ον : (contracts to -ξους, ουν); opposed, adverse; τὸ ἀντίξοον: opposition
ἀντίος, -ία, ίον: opposite, contrary, set against; (+ Gen.) set against, opposite
ἄνω: (Adv.) (With Verbs implying Motion) upwards, up, on the upper side
ἄξιος, -ία, -ιον: worthy, deserving to be
ἀξύνετος, -ον: witless, devoid of understanding, not able to understand
ἀοιδός, -οῦ, ὁ: bard, minstrel, singer
ἀπάγχω: to strangle, choke, hang
ἅπας, ἅπασα, ἅπαν: all, the whole, everything, all together
ἄπειμι: to be absent, to be away, to be far from
ἄπειρος, -ον: without trial, without experience of a thing, unused to, unacquainted to
ἀπεργάζομαι: to finish off, complete
ἀπιστία, -ας, ἡ: unbelief, distrust, disbelief
ἀποθνήσκω: to die
ἀποκαθαίρω: to clear, cleanse
ἀπολείπω: to leave behind, desert
ἀπονίζω: to wash clean, wash off,
ἄπορος, -ον: without passage, impassable, having no way in, hard to discover, hard to solve
ἀποσβέννυμι: to extinguish, quench, go out, vanish, cease, extinguish
ἀποστρέφω: to turn back; to turn aside; to divert
ἄποτος, -ον: not drinkable, not drunk from, never delivering, not drinking, unable to drink
ἅπτω: to kindle, set on fire
ἅπτω: to touch, affect, engage in
ἀρείφατος, -ον: slain by Ares, slain in war
ἀρετὴ, -ῆς, ἡ: virtue, goodness, excellence, merit
ἄριστος, -η, -ον: best, noblest, bravest, most excellent
ἄρκτος, -ου, ἡ: bear; the north; also refers to *Ursa Major*, the constellation
ἁρμονία, -ας, ἡ: harmony, agreement, fastening, covenant, order
ἀρρωστέω (ῶ): to be unwell, ill
ἀρχή, -ῆς, ἡ: beginning, origin
ἀρχηγός, -ά, -όν: chief, prince, captain, lead, primary
Ἀρχίλοχος: Archilochus, lyric poet from Paros
ἄρχω: to rule, govern, command, be leader of; begin
ἀστρολογέω (-ῶ): to study the stars or study astronomy
ἀστρολόγος, -ου, ὁ: someone who studies the stars or astronomy
ἄστρον, -ου, τό: a star
αὐαίνω: to dry, wither, waste away
αὐγὴ, -ῆς, ἡ: light of the sun, sunlight, ray, gleam, sheen
αὖθις: (Adv.) (of time) again, anew; (of place) back, back again; (of future time) hereafter
αὐξάνω: to increase, strengthen, grow, promote
αὐτός, -ή, -όν: (Reflexive Pro.) himself, herself, itself; (pl.) themselves; (Art. + form of αὐτός, -ή, -όν) the same
αὐχμέω (ῶ): to be squalid, to be unwashed
ἀφανὴς, -ές: unseen, unnoticed, out of sight, invisible
ἀφίημι: to send forth, send away, let loose
ἀφικνέομαι: to arrive, reach
βαθὺς, βαθεῖα, βαθύ: deep, profound, high, strong, copious, abundant
βαίνω: to walk, step, go, set out
βακχάω: to be in Bacchant frenzy, rave
βαρβάρος, -α, -ον: foreign, non-Greek, barbarian
βασανίζω: to torture, examine
βασιλεία, -ᾶς, ἡ: kingdom, dominion
βασιλεὺς, βασιλέως, ὁ: king, master, chief, lord, patron
Βίας, Βίαντος, ὁ: Bias; traditionally considered as one of the Seven Wise Men of Ancient Greece.
βιός, -οῦ, ὁ: bow, bowmanship, archery

βίος, -ου, ὁ: life

βλάξ, βλάκος, ὁ, ἡ: stupid, soft, stolid

βόρβορος, -ου, ὁ: filth, mire

βουλή, -ῆς, -ἡ: counsel, determination, advice

γάρ: (Conj.) for, since

γένεσις, -εως, ἡ: birth, origin, beginning, genesis

γενητός, -ή, -όν: originated, generated

γένος, -ους, τὸ: race, stock, kind, class, family, generation, sort, descent, kin

γῆ, γῆς, ἡ: earth, soil, land

γηραιός, -ά, -όν: old, aged

γίγνομαι: become, come into being, be born, be produced

γιγνώσκω: to know, perceive, understand, be aware of

γναφεῖον, -ου, τό: fuller (someone who spins and cleans wool or cloth)

γνώμη, -ης, ἡ: purpose, intention; motion; judgment, opinion, thought; understanding, means of knowing, intelligence, thought, judgement; LSJ takes γνώμας as "practical maxims."

γνῶσις, -εως, ἡ: knowledge,

γοῦν: Compound Particle of γε οὖν; at least then, at all events

δαίμων, -ονος, ὁ/ἡ: god/goddess; LSJ takes this also as "the power controlling destiny of individuals

δέ: (Particle) but, and, but on the other hand, or just leave untranslated

δεῖ: (w/Acc. or Infin.) it is necessary, it is needful for one to do, one must

δείκνυμι: to show, make known, point out, prove, displayed

Δελφοί, -ῶν, οἱ: Delphi

δεινός, ή, όν: powerful, fearful, terrible

Δημόκριτος: Pre-Socratic Philosopher and Physicist; famous along with Leucippus as being an Atomist[lviii]

δῆμος, -ου, ὁ: land, district, country, people, inhabitants, government, township; people, populace

διά: (Prep. + Acc.): through, on account of, because of, by the aid of; (Prep. + Gen.): through, throughout, along

διαγιγνώσκω: to distinguish, discern, determine, know one from the other

διαείδω: to be dissonant

διαιρετός, -ή, -όν: separated, divided, distinguishable

διαιρέω: to take apart, divide into parts; determine, divide among themselves

διαφέρω: differ, struggle, quarrel, to be at variance, to carry in different directions or ways; to be drawn apart, to be disrupted; to differ, carry different ways; to quarrel with, differ with, be at variance with (+Dat.)

διαφεύγω: (alt. form is διαφυγγάνω) to escape, get away from, escape one; notice

διαχέω (ῶ): to liquify, melt, fuse

διδασκάλος, -ου, ὁ: teacher, master, trainer

διδάσκω: to teach, instruct, train

δίζημαι: to seek out, look for, desire; seek the meaning of; seek

διηγέομαι: to set out in detail, describe

διηνεκής, -ές: unbroken, continuous

διίστημι: to set apart, separate, stand apart

δίκαιος, -ία, -ιον: just, righteous, lawful, right,

Δίκη, Δίκης, ἡ: Dike, the goddess of justice, law, order, right, judgment in the past

δίκη, -ας, ἡ: justice, right, order, custom

διὸ: (Conj.) wherefore, on which account

διοικέω: to manage, govern, administer, furnish, control

Διόνυσος, -ου, ὁ: Dionysus, god of revelry and wine

δὶς: (Adv.) twice, doubly

διττός, -ή, -όν: twofold, double

δοκέω (-ῶ): to seem; to think, suppose, imagine, expect

δόκιμος, -η, -ον: trustworthy, esteemed, acceptable, noble, excellent

δόμος, -ου, ὁ: house, dwelling

δόξασμα, δοξάσματος, τό: opinion, notion, conjecture

δοῦλος, -ου, ὁ: slave, bondman, serf

δύω: to sink, plunge, set; (when referring to the sun; sink, set)

ἐάν: if (+Subj.) (+FMV or +PGC)

87

ἑαυτοῦ, -ῆς, -οῦ: (No Nom.) himself, herself, itself
ἐγείρω: to awaken, rouse, stir up
ἐγερτί: (Adv.) busily, eagerly
ἐγκύρω: to encounter, fall in with, meet with, light upon; to meet with (+Gen.)
ἐγρείρω: to awaken, rouse
ἐγώ: I
ἐθέλω: to will to, want to, wish
εἰ: (Conj.) if
εἶδον: to see
εἶδος, -εος, τό: form, kind; (Literally: that which is seen)
εἰκῆ: at random, without plan, without purpose
εἰκότως: (Adv.) suitably, reasonably
εἰμί: I am; Ancient Greek form of verb to be; Latin equivalent *sum*
εἶμι: to go, go in, come, go through, enter
εἶπον: (Aor. 1ˢᵗ. Sg. Ind.) to say, speak
εἰρήνη, -ης, ἡ: peace
εἷς, μία, ἕν: (Gen. ἑνός) one
εἰς: (Prep + Acc.) into, onto, up to, until
εἰσαγωγή, -ῆς, ὁ: magistrate, conduit; (Literally: the bringer in or introducer)
ἐκ: (Prep. + Gen.) out of, from, forth from
ἕκαστος, -η, -ον: each, every
Ἑκαταῖος, -ου, ὁ: Hecataeus; specifically Hecataeus of Miletus (550 BCE – 476 BCE) who was a
ἐκβάλλω: to throw out, banish, cast aside, cast out, throw
ashore, throw aside
ἔκβλητος, -α, -ον: thrown out, cast overboard
ἐκεῖνος, ἐκείνη, ἐκεῖνο: (Demon. Pro.) that there; that; (Pl.) those
ἐλευθέρος, -α, -ον: free, independent
Ἑλλήν: Hellene
ἔλπω: to hope, expect, cause to hope, deem, suppose
ἐμαυτοῦ: (only in Gen., Dat., and Acc.) myself
ἐμβαίνω: to step in, go on, enter, step upon, embark
ἐν: (Prep. + Dat.) in, on, at, among
ζάω (-ῶ): to live
ἐναντίος, -α, -ον: opposite, contrary, reverse
ἕνεκα: (Prep. +Gen.) for the sake of, on account of, for, in consequence of, because
ἔνθα: (Adv.) there, thither
ἐντεῦθεν: (Adv.) hence, from here, thence; from this time, henceforth; therefore
ἐξακέομαι: to heal completely, appease
ἐξαπατάω: to deceive
ἐξαρκέω: to suffice, be enough for
ἐξευρίσκω: find out, discover, invent, search out, search after, procure, win,
ἐξικνέομαι: to arrive, reach, come to (someplace); to complete, accomplish
ἕξις, -εως, ἡ: state, habit
ἔοικα: Perf. Act. form translated in a Pres. Aspect; to seem to, to be like, to be considered like, be analogous
to (+Dat.)
ἐπαιτέω (ῶ): to ask besides, beg, demand
ἐπαίω: to have knowledge of, understand, perceive; listen to
ἐπανίστημι: to set up again, make rise against
ἐπειδάν: whenever (+Subj.)
ἐπέρχομαι: to come upon, come near, come against, come on, return,
ἐπί: (+Dat.) at, on, upon, in; (Prep. + Gen.) in, in the presence of; on, upon, at
ἐπίκουρος, ἐπικούρου, ὁ: ally, friend, protector, assistant, guard
ἐπιλανθάνομαι: to forget
ἐπιπορέομαι: travel
ἐπιρρέω: flow upon, keep flowing, streaming on

ἐπίσταμαι: to know, be able, to be assured, observe, understand; know how to do, be able to, capable to do
ἐπιφράζω: to notice, think to do, contrive
ἕπομαι: to follow, come after, pursue, obey, submit, understand
ἔπος, ἔπους, τὸ: word. (as opposed to deed), speech, poetry, story,
ἐργάζομαι: to work at, labor, make
ἐργάτης, -ου, ὁ: worker, laborer,
ἔργον, -ου, τό: work, deed, industry, labor, action, proper work, business
Ἐρινύες: the Furies; the three Greek female gods of punishment, vengeance, and curses
ἔρις, -ιδος, ἡ: strife, quarrel, debate, contention, battle, fight, contest, disputation
Ἑρμόδωρος, -ου, ὁ: Hermodorus
ἑρπετόν, -οῦ, τό: animal, quadruped, reptile, living being
ἑσπέρα, -ας, ἡ: evening; the west
ἐστίν: 3rd Pres. Act. of εἰμί; he/she/it is
ἕτερος, -α, -ον: other, different, another
ἔτος, -εος, τό: year
εὖ: (Adv.) well
εὐαρίθμητος, -ον: easy to count, few in number
εὕδω: to sleep
εὐθύς, -εῖα, -ύ: straight, direct
εὑρίσκω: to find, discover, happen upon by chance, acquire, obtain, fetch
Εὖρος, -ους, τό: width, breath
εὐφρόνη, -ης, ἡ: night (literally: the kindly time)
εὔχομαι: to pray, long for, wish for, promise, vow
Ἐφέσιος, -α, -ον: Ephesian, native of Ephesus
ἔχω: to have, hold, possess
ζάω (-ῶ): to live
Ζεύς, Διός, ὁ: the god Zeus
Ζεύς, Ζηνὸς, ὁ: Zeus
ἤ: (Conj.) or
ἤ: (with Comp.) than
Ἡ.: Heraclitus
ἡβηδόν: (Adv.) from the youth up
ἥδομαι: to enjoy oneself; to be glad; to delight in; to be amused; to be pleased;
ἡδονή, -ῆς, ἡ: pleasure, delight
ἡδύς, ἡδεῖα, ἡδύ: sweet, pleasant, glad, well-pleased
ἦθος, -εος, τό: disposition, character, custom, usage
ἥλιος, - ου ὁ: sun
ἥλιος, ἡλίου, ὁ: the sun, daylight, sunshine
ἡμεῖς: (Pronoun) we
ἡμέρα, -ας, ἡ: day
ἡμέτερος, -α, -ον: our, ours
ἥμισυς, -υ: half
Ἡράκλειτος: Heraclitus
ἥρως, ἥρωος, ὁ/ἡ: hero
Ἡσίοδος, -ου, ὁ: Hesiod (~700 BC); one of the most famous ancient Greek epic poets; his works
include the *Theogony* and *Works and Days*
ἠώς, ἠοῦς, ἡ: dawn, daybreak; the goddess of dawn, aurora
θάλαττα, -ης, ἡ: sea, sea-water, salt-water
θάνατος, -ου, ὁ: death
θεῖος, -α, -ον: of or from the gods, divine, sacred, holy
θεὸς, -οῦ, ὁ: deity, god, divine
θερμός, -ά, -όν: hot, warm, fresh
θέρος, -εος, τό: summer
θέρω: to heat, make hot, make (+Acc. Obj.) warm
θνήσκω: to die, to be dying
θνητός, -ή, -όν: mortal, human, mortal creature, one liable to death

θυμός, -οῦ: spirit, desire, heart, passion
θυσία, -ας, ἡ: sacrifice, offering, victim
θύωμα, -ατος, τό: something burnt as incense; (Pl.) spices
ἰατρός, -οῦ, ὁ: doctor, physician
ἴδιος, -α, -ον: private, personal, one's own, private, separate, distinct, peculiar
ἱερός, -ά, -όν: holy, divine, hallowed, supernatural
ἴστωρ, -ορος, ὁ: wise man, one who knows right, a judge, or knowing
ἰσχυρίζομαι: to rely on, put trust in (something)
ἰσχυρός, -ά, -όν: strong, powerful
ἰχθύς, ἰχθύος, ὁ: fish
καθαλιρω: to purify, cleanse, wash, purge, evacuate
καθάπερ: (Adv.) exactly as
καθαρός, ά, όν: clean, pure, unmixed, clear
καθεύδω: sleep, lie down to sleep, lie idle, sleep away, pass the night, lie
καί: (Conj.) and, even, also
καίω: to kindle, ignite, set on fire
κακίζω: to abuse, reproach
κακός, -ή, όν: wicked, evil, mean, ugly, ignoble, base, baneful, bad
κάλλος, -ους, τὸ: beauty, nobility, something or somebody beautiful
καλός, -ή, -όν: beautiful, noble, good, fair, genuine, honorable, virtuous, happy
κάματος, -ου, ὁ: toil, trouble, weariness, pain
κάματος, καμάτου, ὁ: weariness, exhaustion, fatigue.
καπνός, καπνοῦ, ὁ: smoke
καρφαλέος, -α, -ον: dry, parched
κατά: (+Acc.) according to, corresponding with, after the fashion of; along, through, downwards
καταβαύζω: to bark at, bark against
κατακτείνω: to kill, slay
καταλαμβάνω: to seize, lay hold of
καταλείπω: to leave behind, forsake, abandon, leave alone
κατευθύνω: to steer, direct, guide
κάτω: (Adv.) (With Verbs implying Motion) downwards, down, below, southward, lower
κεβερνάω (-ῶ): steer, guide, govern, act as pilot, act as a helmsman
κεραυνός, -οῦ, ὁ: thunderbolt
κινέω (ῶ): to set in motion; (Pass./Mid.) to be stirred/moved
κλέος, τό: fame, renown, glory, rumor, report
κοιμάω (ῶ): to sleep; (Mid./Pass.) to be put to sleep
κοινός, -ή, -όν: common, public, ordinary
κόπις, -ιδος, ὁ: liar, wrangler, prater
κόπριον, -ου, τό: dirt, filth
κορέννυμι: to satiate, fill
κόρος, -ου, ὁ: satisfaction, satiety, excess, abundance, surfeit
κόσμος, -ου, ὁ: world, order, universe, earth
κρατέω (ῶ): to rule, hold sway,
κρατύς, -εῖα,-υ: strong, mighty
κρίνω: to separate, put asunder, distinguish, pick out, choose, judge, decide,
κρίσις, -εως, ἡ: decision, judgment, choice
κρύπτω: to hide, cover, conceal, keep secret, suppress, lie hidden
κτηνος, κτήνους, τό: flocks, herds, beast, ox, sheep, horse
κυκάω (ῶ): to stir, mix, confound
κύκλος, -ου, ὁ: circle, ring
κύων, κυνός, ὁ or ἡ: dog (either male or female)
κωφός, -ή, -όν: deaf and dumb, mute, dull, obtuse,
λαγχάνω: to obtain, to obtain by lot, obtain as one's portion
λαμβάνω: to seize, take hold of, grasp; catch, overtake
λανθάνω: to escape notice, escape, pass over

λέγω: say, speak, converse, tell a story
λεσχηνεύω: to chat, converse with
Λῆναι, αἱ: The Bacchanals
ληναίζω: to celebrate Bacchanalian rites
λιμός, -οῦ, ὁ: hunger, famine
λόγος, -ου, ὁ: best to leave it as λόγος (or) as word, account, reason, understanding
λύρα, -ας, ἡ: lyre
Μάγος, -ου, ὁ: Magi, one of the priests of Persia; also, enchanter, wizard, imposter, charlatan
μάθησις, -εως, ἡ: learning, education
μαίνομαι: to rage, be furious, be mad, riot, be mad
μάλα: (Adv.) much, very, exceedingly; (Comp μᾶλλον) more
μάλιστα: (Sup.) best, most, above all
μανθάνω: to learn
μαντεῖόν, τό: oracle, oracular response, seat of an oracle
μαντεύομαι: to divine, prophesy, forbode, presage, surmise, draw divinations, consult an oracle, seek divinations,
μαρτυρέω (ῶ): bear witness; (with Dat. of Person) bear witness to/confirm that something is the case; (with Inf.) give evidence/testify that something is the case
μάρτυς, μάρτυρος, ἡ or ὁ: witness
μάχομαι: to quarrel, dispute, wrangle, contend, compete; (+Dat.) to make war, fight, battle; fight against (+ Dat.)
μέγας, μεγάλη, μέγα: big, great, vast, mighty, strong, important, large, mighty, big, marvelous
μέγεθος, -εος: Ionic for μέγαθος, -ους, τό: greatness, magnitude, size, height, stature,
μεθύσκω: to be drunk, to be intoxicated
μέν: (Particle) indeed; on the one hand, while, whereas, or just leave untranslated
μέν...δέ: on the one hand...on the other hand
μέντοι: (Particle) however, indeed, to be sure
μένω: to stay, remain; wait, await, expect (+Acc or Inf.)
μέσος, -η, -ον: middle, midst, intervening space
μετά: (Prep. + Gen.) with, among, between; (Prep. +Acc.) after, into the middle of, among, in pursuit of, between, afterwards
μεταβάλλω: to turn about, alter, change
μεταβολη, -ῆς, ἡ: change, transformation
μεταπίπτω: to change in form, fall differently
μέτειμι: to be among (lit: "to be with"); to have a part in, or to have a share in
μετρέω (ῶ): to measure, count
μέτρον, -ου, τό: measure, rule, length, space, dimension
μὴ: (Particle) no, not
μηδὲ: (Conj.) and not
μηδείς, μηδεμία, μηδέν: no one, nothing
μήτε...μήτε: (Correl.) neither...nor
μιαίνω: to corrupt, taint, defile, stain, sully
μιαρός, -ά, -όν: polluted, abominable, foul, defiled, repulsive, unclean
μιμνήσκω: to remind, put in mind; (+Gen.) remember, mention
μισθός, οῦ, ὁ: wages, pay
μοῖρα, -ας, ἡ: part, portion, division, degree, share; destiny, lot
μόνος, -η, ον: alone, one, unique
μόρος, -ου, ὁ: fate, destiny
μοῦνον: Ionic form of μόνον; (ADJ.) alone; (ADV.) only, solely
μοχθέω (-ῶ): to be weary, worn with toil, to be sore, to labor
μυέω (ῶ): to initiate or be initiated into the mysteries.
μυρίος, -α, -ον: numberless, countless, infinite, measureless
μυστήριον, -ου, τό: mysteries, referring to the Dionysian Mysteries or rites
μύστης, -ου, ὁ: an initiate
νεκρός, -οῦ, ὁ: corpse, dead body
νέμω: to drive to pasture, tend, pasture
νέος, -η, -ον: new, young, fresh, youthful
νήπιος, -η, -ον: childish, infantile, silly, blind, without foresight

91

νομίζω: to believe, think, esteem, acknowledge
νόμος, -ου, ὁ: practice, law, ordinance, custom, statute
νόος, νόου, ὁ: intelligence, intellect, mind, sense, wit, reason, thought
νόσος, -ου, ἡ: illness, sickness, plague, disease, suffering, madness, distress, bane
νοτίζω: to moisten, to water; (Intrans.) to be wet
νοῦς, νοῦ, ὁ: mind intelligence, wit
νυκτιπόλος, -ον, -η: roaming at night
ξένος, -η, -ον: foreign, strange, unusual
Ξενοφάνης, -ους, ὁ: Xenophanes; specifically Xenophanes of Colophon (570 BCE – 478 BCE)
ξηρός, -ή, -όν: dry, withered, lean
ὁ, ἡ, τό: (Def. Art.) the, that
ὄγος, -ου, ὁ: best to leave it as λόγος (or) as word, account, reason, understanding
ὅδε, ἥδε, τόδε: (Demonstrative) this
ὁδός, -οῦ, ἡ: way, road, path; journey, trip, means, manner, method
ὅθεν: (Adv.) whence
οἰακίζω: to steer, govern, manage, guided
οἶδα: (Pf. Form translated as Present) I know
οἴησις, -εως, ἡ: self-conceit
οἶνος, -ου, ὁ: wine; or cup (presumably to hold wine)
οἴομαι: to think, conjecture, suppose, expect
οἷος, οἵα, οἷον: just as, as; such as
ὁκοῖος, -α, -ον: of what sort, of whatever kind, of what quality
ὁκόταν: (Adv.) whenever, whensoever (+Subj.)
ὅκωσπερ: Ionic, Conj. just as, in such a manner as, as
ὃκωσπερ: just as, as
ὀλέθριος, -ον: destructive, deadly, fatal, bringing ruin
ὀλίγος, -η, -ον: few, little, low, small
ὅλος, -η, -ον: whole, entire, utter, complete in all its parts; all, the whole; (as Neuter Substantive) the universe, all things, everything
Ὅμηρος, -ου, ὁ: Homer
ὁμιλέω: to be in contact with, be acquainted with, associate with
ὅμιλος, -ου, ὁ: crowd, throng, tumult
ὁμοίως: (Adv.) similarly, likewise, unchangingly
ὁμολογεώ (ῶ): to agree with, correspond, agree to, concede, acknowledge, admit, agree to do, promise to do, concede
ὄνειος, -α, -ον: valuable, useful
ὄνομα, ὀνόματος, τό: by name, name
ὀνομάζω: to call, name, specify
ὄνος, -ου, ὁ and ἡ: ass or donkey
ὀξύτης, -ητος, ἡ: sharpness, pointedness
ὅπη: (Adv.) wherever, in any direction/manner, by what way
ὁπόσος, -η, -ον: as many as, as much as; (In Indirect Questions) however much, however many
ὁπόταν: (Adv.) whenever, whensoever (+Subj.)
ὅπως: (Adv.) as, in such manner as, how, just as, that, in the manner of; (Conj.) in order that
ὅρασις, -εως, ἡ: seeing, the act of sight, vision, power of sight
ὁράω (ῶ): to see
ὅρος, -ου, ὁ: boundary, limit, frontier
ὀρύσσω: to dig
ὅς, ἥ, ὅ: (Relative Pronoun) who, which
ὀσμάομαι (ῶμαι): to have a sense of smell; smell
ὅσος, -α, -ον: whatever, what
ὅσος, -η, -ον: (Adj.) how many, as much as, so far as, so many as
ὅστις, ἥτις, ὅτι: whoever, anyone, anything which, whichsoever, whatsoever, anything
ὅτι: that
οὐ: (Particle) no, no, non

οὐδὲ: (Conj.) and not, not yet, but not, nor
οὐδὲ: (Conj.) and not, not yet, but not, nor
οὐδείς, οὐδεμία, οὐδέν: no one, nothing
οὐκ: (Particle) not, no, non
οὖν: certainly, therefore, really, in fact
οὖρος, οὔρου, ὁ: guardian watcher
οὖς, ὠτός, τό: ear
οὐσία, -ας, ἡ: being, substance, essence
οὔτε...οὔτε: (Correl.) neither...nor
οὗτος, αὕτη, τοῦτο: this; (pl.) those, these
οὕτω: (Adv.) in this way, so
οὕτω(ς): (Adv.) so, thus, in this way, in this manner, so much, excessively
ὀφθαλμός, -οῦ, ὁ: eye
οφός, -ή, -όν: wise, prudent, skilled, clever, learned, ingenious, cleverly devised
ὄψις, -εως, ἡ: sight, appearance, aspect; face, vision, act of seeing, looking
παίζω: to play (a game), to play a sport
παῖς, παιδός, ὁ/ἡ: child, kid, son, daughter, boy, girl
πάλιν: (Adv.) again, back
παλίντροπος, -η, -ον: contrary, turned away, averted
παντάπασιν: (Adv.) all in al, altogether, wholly
παρά: (Prep. + Gen) from, beside; (Prep.+ Acc.) beside, over, along, beyond, near, by
παραλαμβάνω: to receive from;
παραπλησίος, -α, -ον: in the same manner, just as, equally
πάρειμι: to be present, to be by, to be near, to be at hand or ready
πᾶς, πασα, πᾶν: all, every, each, whole
πατήρ, πατρός/πατέρος, ὁ: father
πείθω: (Active)persuade, convince; (Middle/Passive) to obey, trust, believe (+Dat.)
πεῖραρ, -ατος, τό: end, limit
πειράω (ῶ): to try, attempt, endeavor (+Gen.)
πέρας, πέρατος, τό: limit, end, boundary
περί: (+Gen.) concerning or about
περιγίγνομαι: to be left over, to remain
περιφέρεια, -ας, ἡ: circumference
πεσσεύω: to play at draughts
πηλὸς, -οῦ, ὁ/ἡ: mud, clay, earth
πίθηκος, -ου, ὁ: ape, monkey, dwarf
πίθηκος, -ου, ὁ: ape, monkey, dwarf
πλεῖστος, -η, -ον: Sup. of πολύς, πολλή, πολύ; most, greatest, largest, greatest number
πλείων, πλεῖον: comparative of πολύς, πολλή, πολύ; more, greater
πληγή, -ῆς, ἡ: stroke, blow, physical strike
ποιέω (-ῶ): make, do, act, produce, cause
πόλεμος, -ου, ὁ: war, conflict, battle
πόλις, -εως, ἡ: polis, city-state
πολυμαθία: much learning or much knowledge
πολύς, πολλή, πολύ: (with nouns of mass/amount) a lot of, much, great amount; many; many, majority, all
(οἱ) πολλοί: the many, the majority, the multitude
πομπὴ, -ῆς, ἡ: solemn procession, parade, escort
ποταμός, -οῦ, ὁ: river, stream
πότε: (Enclitic Particle) at some time, at another time; (Interrogative Particle) ever, at any time, when
πότιμος, -α, -ον: drinkable, fresh
πούς, ποδός, ὁ: a foot
πρηστήρ, -ῆρος, ὁ: hurricane, water spout
Πριήνη, ἡ: Priene; ancient Greek city in Ionia on the western coast of Turkey
πρὸς: (+Acc.) in proportion to, in relation to, in comparison with, over, by; (+Gen) before, in the presence of from, at, to; on the side of, in the direction of

πρόσειμι: to be present, to be at hand
προσεῖπον: to address, speak to, call, name
πρόσθεν: (of Time) before, formerly; (Adv. of Space/Place) before, outside, in front of
προτιμάω (-ῶ): to honor, prefer, wish, take heed of
πρῶτος, -η, -ον: first, foremost, earliest
πτοέω: to dismay, distract, excite, scare, terrify
πτῶσις, -εως, ἡ: falling, fall, arrangement
Πυθαγόρας, -ου, ὁ: Pythagoras; specifically Pythagoras of Samos (; the famous pre-Socratic
πῦρ, πυρός, τό: fire; funeral-fire, sacrificial fire, hearth fire
πυρκαϊά, -ᾶς, ἡ: conflagration, arson, funeral pyre, burning pyre
πῶς: How? (With particles like ἄν or κε, used with the optative_
ῥαπίζω: to strike with a stick, cudgel; slap in the face; beat, strike;
ῥήτωρ, -ορος, ὁ: orator, public speaker, rhetorician
ῥίς, ῥινός, ἡ: nose, nostrils, (or pipes/conduits)
ῥυπάω (ῶ): to be filthy
σάρμα, -ατος, τό: refuse pile, sweepings
σβέννυμι: to quench, put out, dry up, quell, check
σημαίνω: to indicate, show by a sign, point out, give a sign
Σίβυλλα,-ας, ἡ: the Sibyl, prophetess
σκίδνημι: to disperse, spread, scatter
σκολιός, -ά, -όν: bent, curved, crooked
σοφός, -ή, -όν: wise, prudent, skilled, clever, learned, ingenious, cleverly devised
σπανίος, -α, -ον: rare, scant, scarce
στόμα, -ατος, τό: mouth, face
σύλληψις, -εως, ἡ: inclusion, taking together, comprehension, conception, summing up
συμβάλλω: conjecture, infer, conclude, interpret; *Literally*: to throw together (+Dat)
συμμίγνυμι: to mix together, commingle:
συμφέρω: to come together, collect, bring together, gathering; is in harmony with, harmonize, occur, unite, gather, collect
συμφορά, -ῆς, ἡ: misfortune, punishment, disease
σύν: (Prep. + Dat.) with
συνάγω: to bring together, gather together
συνάδω: to be in accord with, agree with,
συνεργός, -ά, -όν: working together, joining; (+Gen.) taking part in
συνεχής, -ές: contiguous, continuous, unremitting, constant
συνίημι: to understand, observe, notice (*lit*: "to send together")
σύρμα, -ατος, τό: refuse, trash, sweepings
σφάλλω: (when describing drunken behavior) to reel, to stagger
σωτήριος, -ον: saving, delivering, bringing safety
τάχος, -εος, τό: swiftness
τε: (Conj.) and, also, but or untranslated
τε...καί: both...and
τεῖχος, τείχους, ὁ: city, mound, wall, fortification, fortress
τέκτων, ονος, ὁ: maker, craftsman, workman, author, master
τέμνω: to cut, wound, maim
τέρμα, -ατος, τό: end, boundary, limit
τέρψις, -εως, ἡ: enjoyment, pleasure, delight
τίθημι: to set, set up, assign, reckon
τιμάω (-ῶ): honor, hold in honor, revere, treat honorably, pay honorably
τίς, τίς, τί: (Interrogative Pro.) who?, what?, what kind?
τις, τι, (Gen.: τινος): anyone, anything, someone, something
τοίνυν: therefore, accordingly, then
τοιοῦτος, τοιαύτη, τοιοῦτο: this sort or kind
τοκεύς, -έως, ὁ: parent
τόξον, -ου, τό: bow

τοσοῦτος, τοσαύτη, τοσοῦτο: so large, so many, so much
τότε: (Adv.) then, at that time
τρέφω: to nourish, feed, sustain
τροπή, -ῆς, ἡ: turn, change
ἐθέλω: to will, want, wish
ὕβρις, ὕβρεως, ἡ: insolence, wanton violence, outrage
ὑγίεια, ὑγιείας, ἡ: health
ὑγρός, - ά, -όν: wet, moist, fluid
ὕδωρ, ὕδατος, τό: water
υἱός, -οῦ, ὁ: son
ὑμνέω: to sing, praise in sing, hymn
ὑπέρ: (Prep. + Gen.) over, on behalf of, in defense of, for the safety of, for the prosperity of
ὑπερβαίνω: to step over, transgress, go beyond, overstep, surpass
ὕπνος, -ου, ὁ: sleep, rest, slumber
ὑπό: (Prep. + Gen. of Cause/Agent) by
ὑπολαμβάνω: to suppose, to assume, to suspect
ὗς, ὑός, ὁ or ἡ: pig, swine, hog
φαίνω: (+ Pred. Adj.) appear, come into being, bring to light, shows, displays
φανερός: visible, manifest, evident, apparent
φάος, -εος, τό: light, daylight, day
φάσκω: to think, say, affirm, assert
φάτις, ἡ: saying, proverb, voice from heaven, an oracle
φέρω: to bring, bear, convey, produce, bring forward
φημί: to say, speak, agree
φθέγγομαι: to utter, rave, shout loudly, cry out, proclaim
φθείρ, φθειρός, ὁ: louse; (pl.) lice
φιλέω (-ῶ): to love, like, approve, to be fond of
φιλόσοφος, -ου, ὁ: Literally: philosopher; lover of wisdom, one who speculates on truth and reality
φιλόσοφος, -η, -ov: philosophic
φράζω: to show, point out, make known, explain, declare, tell, indicate
φρήν, φρενός, ἡ: heart, mind, imagination
φρονέω (ῶ): to think, to have understanding, be wise, be prudent
φρόνησις, -εως, ἡ: practical wisdom, thought
φύλαξ, -ακος, ὁ: guard, watcher, sentry
φυλάσσω: to keep watch and ward, keep guard, watch, defend, guard
φύσις, φύσεως, ἡ: nature, origin, birth, shape, form, kind
φωνή, -ῆς, ἡ: voice, speech, utterance, sound
χαίρω: to rejoice, to be glad, take pleasure in, delight in
χαλεπός, -ή, -όν: difficult, hard, grievous
χειμών, -ῶνος, ὁ: winter, cold, frost
χέω: to pour, scatter, shed, drop
χίλιοι, -αι, -α: (Always Pl.) thousand(s)
χράομαι: to use, regard, treat (+Dat.)
χρεών, τό: necessity, fate, that which must be, that which is right, that which is expedient
χρή: (Impersonal +Inf.) it is necessary, one must, one ought, it must needs
χρῆμα, -ατος, τό: property, good, thing, matter
χρησμοσύνη, -ης, ἡ: poverty, need, want
χρυσός, -οῦ, ὁ: gold coin, gold
χωρίζω: to separate, divide, distinguish
ψεῦδος, -εος, τό: lie, falsehood, deceit, fallacy
ψεύδω: to cheat, deceive, beguile, balk, disappoint; (Pass.) to be deceived, to be cheated
ψυχή, -ῆς, ἡ: soul, spirit, mind, life, ghost
ψυχρός, -ά, -όν: cold
ψύχω: to cool, make cold, make cool
ὤν, ὄντος: (Part.) present participle of εἰμί

ὤν, οὖσα, ὄν: Present Part. of εἰμί: being, existing, is
ὠνέομαι: to buy, purchase, bid for
ὡς: (Adv.) as, just as, so, thus, when,
ὥρα, -ας, ἡ: season, period, part of the year
ὥσπερ: (Adv. of Manner) just as, even as, like as,
ὥστε: (Adv.) so as, as being, inasmuch as

Printed in Great Britain
by Amazon

36706790R00055